MANAGEMENT BY OBJECTIVES (MBO) IN ENTERPRISES

Management By Objectives (MBO) in Enterprises

Copyright©: 2011-2018
Dr. W. A. Khan
ISBN: 9781791670559

Published by:

Dr. W. A. Khan
Uxbridge, London
First Edition – 2018
ISBN: 9781791670559

BOOKS IN SEARCH OF MANAGEMENT EXCELLENCE SERIES

1. TOWARDS UNDERSTANDING MANAGEMENT, MANAGEMENT PRINCIPLES AND PROCESS
2. ROLE OF STRATEGIC MANAGEMENT IN BUSINESS ORGANIZATIONS
3. MANAGERIAL ROLES, SKILLS AND COMPETENCIES IN BUSINESS ORGANIZATIONS
4. CREATIVE THINKING, PROBLEM SOLVING AND MANAGERIAL DECISION MAKING
5. ROLE OF DELEGATION IN MANAGEMENT EXCELLENCE OF BUSINESS ORGANIZATIONS
6. **MANAGEMENT BY OBJECTIVES (MBO) IN ENTERPRISES**
7. TIME AND SELF MANAGEMENT FOR EXECUTIVE EXCELLENCE
8. FUNDAMENTALS OF STRESS MANAGEMENT AND JOB BURN-OUT
9. FUNDAMENTALS OF ORGANISZATION PLANNING, DESIGN AND DEVELOPMENT
10. ROLE OF LEADERSHIP IN MANAGEMENT EXCELLENCE

Table of Contents

FOREWORD 7

Chapter 1.. 10
  INTRODUCTION 10

Chapter 2.. 20
  TOWARDS UNDERSTANDING 'MBO' 20
  2.1   INTRODUCTION
  2.2   WHAT IS 'MBO'?
  2.3   CONCEPTS OF 'MBO'
  2.4   UNIQUE FEARURES AND ADVANTAGES OF 'MBO'
  2.5   LEVELS AND DOMAINS OF MBO
  2.6   PRACTICAL CONSIDERATION OF MBO
  2.7   LIMITATIONS OF MBO
  2.8   ARGUMENTS AGAINST MBO
  2.9   CONCLUDING REMARKS

Chapter 3... 31
  TOWARDS UNDERSTANDING 'MBO' PROCESS 31
  3.1   INTRODUCTION
  3.2   PETER DRUCKER'S FIVE-STEP PROCESS FOR 'MBO'
  3.3   ESSENTIAL ELEMENTS OF 'MBO' MODEL

Chapter 4... 37
  THEORY, PRINCIPLES AND PROCESS FOR GOALS
SETTING 37
  4.1   INTRODUUCTION
  4.2   DEVELOPMENTS IN GOAL SETTING THEORY
  4.3   DERIVING GOAL SETTING USING TEMPORAL
        MOTIVATION THEORY
  4.4   LIMITATIONS OF GOAL SETTING THEORY
  4.5   SELECTION OF OBJECTIVES
  4.6   SELECTION OF OBJECTIVES
  4.7   GUIDELINES FOR DEVELOPING GOALS/OBJECTIVES
  4.8   GOAL SETTING IN BUSINESS
  4.9   RELATIONSHIP OF GOAL–PERFORMANCE
  4.10 REALTIONSHIP OF EMPLOYEE MOTIVATION WITH

GOAL SETTING
4.11   IMPACT OF FEEDBACK ON GOAL SETTING
4.12   GOAL SETTING PROCESS

Chapter 5.. **54**
**DEVELOPMENT OF ORGANIZATIONAL GOALS AND
OBJECTIVES** **54**
5.1   INTRODUCTION
5.2   MANAGEMENT OBJECTIVES
5.3   PERFORMANCE OBJECTIVES
5.4   CONCLUDING REMARKS

Chapter 6.. **60**
PERFORMANCE APPRAISAL AND FEEDBACK **60**
6.1   INTRODUCTION
6.2   VERIFIABLE MEASURES
6.3   RESULT-ORIENTED PERFORMANCE
6.4   SELF-CONTROL
6.5   PERFORMANCE FEEDBACK
6.6   CONTINUOUS FEEDBACK

Chapter 7.. **64**
**EVLOLUTION OF MBO: FROM MBO TO BALANCED
SCORECARD**..**64**
7.1   INTRODUCTION
7.2   TIMELINE OF EVOLUTION OF MANAGEMENT BY
OBJECTIVES
7.3   FIFTY (50) YEARS APPRAISAL OF MBO
7.4   CONCLUDING REMARKS

Chapter 8.. **92**
**OTHER MANAGEMENT SYSTEMS CLOSELY RELATED TO
MBO** **92**
8.1   MANAGEMENT BY PARTICIPATION (MBP)
8.2   MANAGEMENT BY FEEDBACK (MBF)
8.3   MANAGEMENT BY WALKING AROUND (MBWA)
8.4   THEORY Z
8.5   MANAGEMENT BY EXCEPTION (MBE)

Chapter 9 .... **101**
MBO AND STRATEGIC MANAGEMENT **101**

9.1   INTRODUCTION

9.2   MANAGEMENT BY OBJECTIVES (MBO) AS A
        MANAGEMENT TOOL
9.3   CONCLUDING REMARKS

Chapter 10.. **122**
  SOME ROAD BLOCKS ENCOUNTERED IN 'MBO'
SYSTEM **122**

Chapter 11.. **125**
  SUMMARY AND CONCLUSION **125**

BIBLIOGRAPHY **129**

FOREWORD

The specific purpose of the "In Search of Management series" is to provide comprehensive knowledge, skills, and know-how to students perusing their studies, and for those who are engaged on potential managerial positions in general and fields of management/administration and allied subjects in particular. The series in its totality will provide guideline to all managers at all level from foreman to chief executive engaged in all industries, trade and commerce.

This book is No.6 in the series: "In Search of management Excellence". The book consists of 10 chapters.

Chapter 1 consists of introduction. Chapter 2 consists of 'Towards Understanding 'MBO' and include: Introduction; What Is 'MBO'? Concepts Of 'MBO'; Unique Features And Advantages Of 'MBO'; Levels And Domains Of MBO; Practical Consideration Of MBO; Limitations Of MBO; Arguments Against MBO; Concluding Remarks. Chapter 3 consists of 'Towards Understanding 'MBO' Process' and include: Introduction; Peter Drucker's Five-Step Process for 'MBO'; and Essential Elements of 'MBO' Model. Chapter 4 consists of 'Theory, Principles And Process For Goals Setting' and include: Introduction; Developments In Goal Setting Theory; Deriving Goal Setting Using Temporal Motivation Theory; Limitations Of Goal Setting Theory; Selection Of Objectives; Selection Of Objectives; Guidelines For Developing Goals/Objectives; Goal Setting In Business; Relationship Of Goal–Performance ; Relationship Of Employee Motivation With Goal Setting; Impact Of Feedback On Goal Setting; and Goal Setting Process. Chapter 5 consists of 'Development of Organizational Goals and Objectives' and include: Introduction; Management Objectives; Performance Objectives; and Concluding

Remarks.

Chapter 6 consists of 'Performance Appraisal and Feedback' and include: Introduction; Verifiable Measures; Result-Oriented Performance; Self-Control; Performance Feedback; and Continuous Feedback. Chapter 7 consists of 'Evolution of MBO: From MBO to Balanced Scorecard' and include: Introduction; Timeline of Evolution of Management by Objectives; Fifty (50) Years Appraisal of MBO; and Concluding Remarks. Chapter 8 consists of 'Other Management Systems Closely Related to MBO' and include: Management by Participation (MBP); Management by Feedback (MBF); Management by Walking around (MBWA); Theory Z; and Management by Exception (MBE). Chapter 9 consists of 'MBO and Strategic Management' and include: Introduction; Management by Objectives (MBO) As a Management Tool; and Concluding Remarks. Chapter 10 consists of 'Some Road Blocks Encountered In 'MBO' System'. Chapter 11 consists of Summary and Conclusion. The book is supported with bibliography.

However, this book is not intended to be the last word. If the reader wishes to gain a further comprehensive knowledge and deep understanding of the subject matters, he or she is directed to consult scholastic work listed under bibliography and the author feels great pleasure in acknowledging his gratitude to all the authors and publishers of this scholastic work which sometimes consulted and quoted in the text of this book. The author earnestly hopes that the matters raised in this book will help the general readers and academic students and scholars and other professional in understanding concepts and application of management, management principles and management process. Finally, the readers and the users of this book are cordially invited to point out errors/mistakes and forward their comments/suggestions, which may bring about improvement to the next edition of this publication.

Praised be to Allah, the Lord of the Worlds!

Dr Wazir Ali Khan
Senior Citizen of Pakistan and the United Kingdon
Advocate of Peace and Social Reforms Activist
Research Scientist, Author and Publisher
Uxbridge (85) UB7 8AB, London, United Kingdom
Email: drwakhan@aol.com
Published Books link:
http://www.amazon.co.uk/s/ref=nb_sb_noss?url=searc
h-alias%3Ddigital-text&field-keywords=Wazir+Khan

Chapter 1

INTRODUCTION

Management has been described as a social process involving responsibility for economical and effective planning and regulation of operation of an enterprise in the fulfillment of given purposes. It is the process of working through individuals and groups to accomplish organizational goals and objectives. It is a dynamic process consisting of various elements and activities, where these activities are different from operative functions like marketing, finance, purchase etc. Rather these activities are those which are common to each and every manger irrespective of his level or status. The management process, by and large, consists of four primary functions, namely: planning, organizing, leading/motivating/directing, and controlling.

Different experts have classified differently functions of management. According to George & Jerry, "There are four fundamental functions of management i.e. planning, organizing, actuating and controlling". According to Henry Fayol, "To manage is to forecast and plan, to organize, to command, & to control". Whereas Luther Gullick has given a keyword 'POSDCORB' where P stands for Planning, O for Organizing, S for Staffing, D for Directing, Co for Co-ordination, R for reporting , and B for Budgeting. The most widely accepted functions are: Planning, Organizing, Staffing, Directing and Controlling as given by koontz and O'Donnel. For theoretical purposes, it may be convenient to separate the function of management but practically these functions are overlapping in nature i.e. they are highly inseparable as each function blends into the other and each affects the performance of others.

It is the basic function of management as it deals with chalking out a future course of action and deciding in advance the most appropriate course of actions for achievement of pre-determined goals. According to Koontz, "Planning is deciding in advance - what to do, when to do & how to do. It bridges the gap from where we are and where we want to be". A plan is a future course of actions. It is an exercise in problem solving and decision making. Planning is determination of courses of action to achieve desired goals. Thus, planning is a systematic thinking about ways and means for accomplishment of pre-determined goals. Planning is necessary to ensure proper utilization of human and non-human resources. It is all pervasive, it is an intellectual activity and it also helps in avoiding confusion, uncertainties, risks, wastages etc.

In its simplest form planning is the thinking that precedes doing. It means determining an organization's goals/ objectives and preparing plans and schedules to achieve them. Decision making (a part of planning process) involves selecting a course of action from a set of alternatives. Therefore, planning and decision making combined is task of determining courses of action to achieve the desired goals. Planning and decision making helps maintain management effectiveness by serving as guides for future activities. Knowing where the manager wants his organization to be at a given time in the future, the manager develops a strategy for getting there. This development process is called strategic planning. Important elements in planning include but not limited to the following:

> Identifying and interpreting goals and objectives passed down from higher level of management.

➢ Collating the ideas/thoughts of the employees directly involved in the work activities.
➢ Formulating policies and procedures to accomplish the desired goals and objectives and making recommendation for their implementation.
➢ Appraising alternatives and selecting suitable activities and programs that will lead to successful results.
➢ Preparing schedules and establishing completion targets.
➢ Determining performance and progress monitoring standards.
➢ Identify resources to accomplish the assigned tasks.

Organizing is the next phase of management process. It is the process of bringing together: physical; financial; and human resources and developing productive relationship amongst them for achievement of organizational goals. According to Henry Fayol: "To organize a business is to provide it with everything useful for its functioning i.e. raw material, tools, capital and personnel". To organize a business involves determining and providing human and non-human resources to the organizational structure. After workable plan is developed through the process of planning and decision making, the next step is to organize the manpower and other resources including capital, equipment, raw materials, facilities, etc. to carry out the plan in the most productive way. Important elements in organizing include but not limited to the following:

➢ Identification of activities.
➢ Assessing availability of sufficient manpower and adequate staffing to accomplish the goals and objectives.

➤ Classification of grouping of activities.
➤ Delineating responsibility and authority at all levels of the organization.
➤ Designing organization and its structure i.e. aligning of major functions and structuring into effective work units/teams by considering both line as well as staff functions etc., and formulating organization charts.
➤ Assignment of duties and preparing job description.
➤ Preparing manuals and administrative guidelines to communicate at all levels, how responsibility and authority has been delineated. Delegation of authority and creation of responsibility.
➤ Preparing a communication system for reporting.
➤ Formulating methods and procedures for problem solving and resolution of conflicts.
➤ Organizing facilities and equipment needed to accomplish assigned tasks.
➤ Coordinating authority and responsibility relationships.

Staffing has assumed greater importance in the recent years due to advancement of technology, increase in size of business, complexity of human behavior etc. It is the function of manning the organization structure and keeping it manned. The main purpose of staffing is to put right man on right job i.e. square pegs in square holes and round pegs in round holes. According to Kootz & O'Donell, "Managerial function of staffing involves manning the organization structure through proper and effective selection process, appraisal and development of personnel to fill the roles designed under the structure". Staffing involves:

- Manpower Planning (estimating man power in terms of searching, choose the person and giving the right place).
- Recruitment, selection & placement.
- Training & development.
- Remuneration.
- Performance appraisal.
- Promotions & transfer.

Leading is that part of managerial function which actuates the organizational methods to work efficiently for achievement of organizational purposes. It is considered life-spark of the enterprise which sets it in motion the action of people because planning, organizing and staffing are the mere preparations for doing the work. Direction is that inert-personnel aspect of management which deals directly with influencing, guiding, supervising, motivating sub-ordinate for the achievement of organizational goals. Direction has following elements: Supervision; Motivation; Leadership; and Communication

Supervision: implies overseeing the work of subordinates by their superiors. It is the act of watching & directing work & workers.

Motivation: means inspiring, stimulating or encouraging the sub-ordinates with zeal to work. Positive, negative, monetary, non-monetary incentives may be used for this purpose.

Leadership: may be defined as a process by which manager guides and influences the work of subordinates in desired direction.

Communications: is the process of passing

information, experience, opinion etc from one person to another. It is a bridge of understanding.

This is the next phase of management after organizing. It is not enough to put people into various slots and expect that everything will take care of itself. Leading/ is most important and perhaps the hardest part of management process. Leading is the set of process used to get members of the organization to work together as a team to further the interest of the organization. Important elements in leading/directing include but not limited to the following:

> Motivating employees to expand efforts. This element includes recognizing employees contribution, delegating authority to make decisions, and creating an environment in which employees can also meet their needs whilst meeting the needs of their organization.
> Instituting participative management and management by objectives, if appropriate.
> Applying appropriate leadership style which focuses on what the manager does to encourage organizational performance.
> Effectively dealing with group and group processes.
> Instituting effective communication.
> Instituting training and human resources development to achieve higher level of motivation resulting in improved performance.

Controlling is the final phase of management process and involves monitoring progress and evaluating activities by setting standards and checklists for evaluating work against these standards, sampling the work flow, and collecting feedback, etc. Controlling implies measurement of accomplishment against the standards and correction of deviation if any to ensure achievement of organizational goals. The purpose of controlling is to ensure that everything occurs in conformities with the standards. An efficient system of control helps to predict deviations before they actually occur. According to Theo Haimann, "Controlling is the process of checking whether or not proper progress is being made towards the objectives and goals and acting if necessary, to correct any deviation". According to Koontz & O'Donell: "Controlling is the measurement and correction of performance activities of subordinates in order to make sure that the enterprise objectives and plans desired to obtain them as being accomplished".

Controlling helps to ensure the effectiveness and efficiency needed for successful management. Important elements in controlling include but not limited to the following:

- ➢ Formulating ways and means to assess whether goals, objectives, or standards have been met in a timely and cost effective manner.
- ➢ Establishing of standard performance.
- ➢ Devising methods and procedures by which the use of the various resources can be measured and evaluated.
- ➢ Perforating measurement of actual performance.
- ➢ Establishing feedback systems to monitor main milestones as the work progresses.
- ➢ Making comparison of actual performance with the standards and finding out deviation if any.
- ➢ Taking corrective action.
- ➢ Reporting the status of work and/or project activities to the management

After describing the various functions of management, we will show herein, how these functions are best performed to achieve excellence in management. 'Management by Objective', generally known as 'MBO' is one of the modern management tools to achieve excellence.

Management by objective was first publicized by Peter Drucker in his book "The Practice of Management" Published in 1954, though this concept was used by Du Port in the early 1920s George S. Odiorne in 1960s endorsed Peter Drucker MBO approach in his book management by objectives published in 1961. Over the years MBO has grown to be quite popular especially in large organizations and is considered a successful tool for integrating participation and control. It has also called much attention to the role of planning and setting objectives.

The method (something called management by results or joint target setting) seems to offer great promise to technical managers seeking increase in their division's effectiveness. Consequently it has produced highly satisfactory results in many organizations. It is appropriate here to cite Harold Koonty following words:

"Perhaps the most powerful tool of managing that has so far been put into practice is the system of managing by objectives. It is simple common sense in that it is a reflection of managing itself. Without clear goals, managing is haphazard and random and no group or individual can expect to perform effectively".[1]

The "Management by Objective" (MBO) approach, in the sense that it requires all managers to set specific objectives to be achieved in the future and encourages them to continually ask what more can be done, and the most important tool the managers have in setting and

---

[1] Koontz, Harold.- *'Shortcomings and Pitfall in Managing by Objectives'*/ Management By Objectives, Jan. 1972, p6.

achieving forward-looking goals is people, the most important asset. In order to achieve results with this tool the manager must: (a) be able to instil in the workers a sense of vital commitment and desire to contribute to organizational goals; (b) control and coordinate the efforts of the workers toward goal accomplishment; and (c) help their subordinates to grow in ability so that they can make greater contributions to the success of the enterprise.

In traditional management approach, most planning and objective setting to achieve these common organizational goals is directed downward, i.e. plans and objectives are passed down from one managerial level to another, and subordinates are told what to do and what they will be held responsible for. Contrary to this approach, the MBO approach injects an element of dialogue into the process of passing plans and objectives from one organizational level to another, where the manager brings specific goals and measures for the subordinate to a meeting with this subordinate, who also brings specific objectives and measures that he/she sees as appropriate or contributing to better accomplishment of the job, and together they develop a group of specific goals, measures of achievement, and time frames in which the subordinate commits her/himself to the accomplishment of those goals. Only then the subordinate is held responsible for the accomplishment of the goals. Bothe, the manager and the subordinate may have occasional progress reviews and revaluation meetings, but at the end of the set period of time, the subordinate is judged on the performance results he/she has achieved. Following this, the subordinate may be rewarded for success by way of salary increase, and/or promotion for good performance or in case of poor performance, he/she may be moved sideways to a job that will be provided needed training or may even be fired from the job. Whatever the outcome, it will be based on the accomplishment of the goals the subordinate had participated in setting and agreed/committed herself/ himself to achieving.

No matter what form it takes in a given organization, MBO is essentially a process that helps to (a) direct managers' attention toward results, (b) force members of the organization to commit themselves to specific achievement, and (c) facilitate their thinking in terms of their organization's future needs and the setting of objectives to meet those needs. Also, the MBO approach can supply the manager with greater measures of three of the tools he or she needs to make the best use of the organization's greatest resource: people, namely: (a) gain greater commitment and desire to contribute from subordinates; (b) gain better control and coordination towards goal accomplishment; and (c) gain an increased ability to help sub-ordinates develop. However, due care must be given as MBO easily can be misused and often is.

For example, what is supposed to be a system that allows for dialogue and growth between boss and subordinate with a view to achieving results may degenerate into a system in which the manager puts constant pressure on the subordinate to produce results and forgets about using MBO for side's commitment, desire to contribute, and management development. The researchers have found that sometimes even well intentioned managers misuse MBO because they do not have the interpersonal skills or knowledge of human needs to keep their performance appraisal sessions from becoming critical. Also, many managers have a tendency to see MBO as a total system that, once installed, can handle all management problems.

Chapter 2

TOWARDS UNDERSTANDING 'MBO'

2.1   INTRODUCTION

In a research study conducted in the late 1970s, 300 American personnel managers were asked to identify in ranks six widely known management tools whose proper application would increase organization effectiveness.[2] 165 personnel managers identified and ranked six tools (including mean values), namely: (i) Management By Objectives (MBO), (ii) Human Relation Training (as a part of formalized management development), (iii) Management Information System (MIS), (iv) Skill Training (as a part of the personnel development program), (v) performance evaluation and review technique; and (vi) Human Resource Accounting. The research finding revealed that 'MBO' was clearly the preferred tool.

2.2   WHAT IS 'MBO'?

Management by Objectives (MBO) is a process of identifying objectives in a company with the intention that management and employees agree to the objectives and know what they have to do within the organization. It is a style of management of an organization which emphasizes the achievement of results expressed in terms of objectives. According to George S. Odiorne, the

---

[2] Peters, Tom, and Nancy Austin.- 'A Passion for Excellence: The Leadership Difference'/ New York: Random House, 1985.

system of management by objectives can be described as a process whereby the superior and subordinate jointly identify its common goals, define each individual's major areas of responsibility in terms of the results expected of him, and use these measures as guides for operating the unit and assessing the contribution of each of its members.[3] MBO is a process of defining objectives within an organization so that management and employees agree to the objectives and understand what they need to do in the organization in order to achieve them. The essence of MBO is: participative goal setting; choosing course of actions; and making decisions. An important part of the MBO is the measurement and the comparison of the employee's actual performance with the standards set, as when employees themselves have been involved with the goal setting and choosing the course of action to be followed by them, they are more likely to fulfill their responsibilities efficiently and diligently.

In MBO process both supervisor and subordinate jointly set overall organizational goals and define each individual's area of responsibility in terms of the expected results. These measures are then used as guidelines for operating the respective organizational unit and also performance appraisal of its members. However, there is a strong constraint attached to the MBO process that objectives must be specific, time bound, realistic, quantitative, qualitative and measurable. In essence, MBO emphasis the importance of subordinates' setting specific objectives, with the help and concurrence of their supervisors, that are intended to be achieved within the period mutually decided upon, and then having their performance measured against the preset objectives.

---

[3] Odiorne, George S., "Management by Objectives; a System of Managerial Leadership", New York: Pitman Pub., 1965.

2.3   CONCEPTS OF 'MBO'

'MBO' is based on certain concepts and hypothesis some of these are as follows:

➢ People prefer to be evaluated according to the standards they perceive to be realistic and reasonably attainable.
➢ If a person is strongly attached to a goal, he/she will be willing to expend more effort to reach a goal than if he/she is less committed to it.
➢ If we predict that something will happen, we will expend every effort to make it happen.

Since, under this method people participate in setting the objectives (or goals) and also in identifying the criteria for performance appraisal, therefore, it tends to incorporate the better parts of several motivational theories (e.g. Maslow's self-fulfillment need; McClelland's need for achievement, McGregor theory 'Y', Herzberg's motivational factors, etc.).

2.4   UNIQUE FEARURES AND ADVANTAGES OF 'MBO'

George Odiorne has explained the values of MBO on various aspects such as: (i) without a pre-set goal, you have no idea whether or not you are on the right path; (ii) you cannot make accurate assessment of results without some prior expectations against which to measure them, (iii) if you are not clear what goal would comprise "non-drifting" or purposive activity, you would not know when thing are drifting, and (iv) if you don't know what goals the organization is seeking (and why) or how well you are doing in relation to these goals, you cannot perform with maximum effectiveness.[4]

Research of Robert H. Mills in an engineering & research environment, has identified that a direct relationship existed between experiencing ambiguity and job tension, personal ineffectiveness, job dissatisfaction and unfavorable attitude towards work associates; and suggest that to reduce these industrial ailments, a program of MBO would be appropriate.[5] Because MBO is based on better communication, co-operation and participation by all levels in the organization, it can realize benefits to all organizational participants; this is why it is often welcomed by both managers and subordinates alike.

MBO is behavioral approach to management in which emphasis is placed more on relationships, than positions and information flow is both ways (unlike conventional approach in which information flow is priority downward and emphasis is on positions rather than relationships). Therefore, MBO approach provides a better co-ordination among various organizational units and leads to better understanding between the superiors and the subordinates.

MBO permits authority to be strengthened (contrary to belief of some managers that participative management system might erode their authority) by developing consent among the subordinates. Because in MBO approach the superior and the subordinates are in agreement on the objectives to be reached, planning is more consistent (against sporadic in traditional

---

[4] Odiorne, George.- 'MBO II: A System of Managerial Leadership for the 80s'/ Belmont, California: Fearson Pitman Publishers, Inc. 1979.

[5] Mills, Robert H.- 'How Job Conflict and Ambiguity Affect R & D Professionals'/ Research Management, Vol. XVIII, No. 4, July 1975.

management), and decisions are more co-operative (against autocratic in traditional management) resulting in much greater motivation and commitment to accomplishment.

According to Martin & Shell, MBO implementation can provide the type of environment where there is both freedom and a strong sense of decision.[6] They have identified and grouped fifteen advantages for an engineering department under three groups namely: (i) for the organization, (ii) for the engineering superior, and (iii) for the subordinates having five advantages under each group[7]. The advantages are as follows:

For the Organization: Advantages include (i) clear goals, (ii) forces planning and control, (iii) surfaces conflicts, (iv) obtain commitment from supervisors, and (v) draws upon first-echelon expertise.

For the Engineering Supervisors: Advantages include: (i) forces effective delegation, (ii) increases time for managing, (iii) two-way communication, (iv) better evaluation criteria, and (v) obtains commitments from subordinates.

For the Subordinates: Behind the principle of Management by Objectives (MBO) is for subordinates to have a clear understanding of the roles and responsibilities expected of them. Then they can understand how their activities relates to the

---

[6] Martin, Desmond D. and Richard L. Shell.- 'What Every Engineer should know about Human Resources Management'/ New York: Marcel Dekker, Inc.

[7] Maslow, Abraham.- 'Euprychian Management: A Journal'/ Homewood, Illinois: Richard D. Brown Inc., 1965, pp. 150.

achievement of the organization's goal. Also places importance on fulfilling the personal goals of each employee. Some of the important features and advantages of MBO are:

1. Motivation – Involving employees in the whole process of goal setting and increasing employee empowerment, and increases employee job satisfaction and commitment.
2. Participation – Allows subordinates' participation
3. Autonomy – It provides autonomy.
4. Better communication and coordination – Frequent reviews and interactions between superiors and subordinates helps to maintain harmonious relationships within the organization and also to solve many problems.
5. Clarity of goals and improves direction and guidance
6. Subordinates tend to have a higher commitment to objectives they set for themselves than those imposed on them by another person.
7. Managers can ensure that objectives of the subordinates are linked to the organization's objectives.
8. Morale – it improves morale of the subordinates.
9. Feedback – It forces feedback from the above.

According to Willian D. Hitt, MBO is a comprehensive approach to management (as again a narrow view held by many managers that it is only a tool for performance appraisal) that applies to all of the managerial functions namely: planning, organizing, staffing, motivating and controlling.[8] For planning function, it forces plan. For organizing, it clarifies roles & responsibilities and provides direction for how the

---

[8] Hitt, William D.- 'Management in Action: Guidelines for New Managers'/ Columbus, Ohio: Battlelle Press, 1984.

enterprise should be organized. For staffing function, it provides guidelines for what kind of people are needed and what kind of knowledge and skills should be developed. For motivating function, it provides direction for employee motivation and brings out commitment for performance. For controlling, it provides milestone and standards for performance evaluation.

2.5   LEVELS AND DOMAINS OF MBO

Objectives can be set at all levels and in all domains of activities, such as: production; services; marketing; sales; research and development (R&D); Information systems; human resources; and finance; etc. Some objectives are collective, for a whole department or the whole company, whilst others can be individualized.

2.6   PRACTICAL CONSIDERATION OF MBO

Objectives need quantifying and monitoring. to establish relevant objectives and monitor their "reach ratio" in an objective way, Reliable management information systems are needed. Pay incentives (i.e. bonuses) are often linked to results in reaching the objectives.

2.7   LIMITATIONS OF MBO

There are several limitations to the base underlying the impact of managing by objectives, which include, but not limited to, the following:

> ➢ It over-emphasizes the setting of goals over the working of a plan as a driver of outcomes.

➤ It underemphasizes the importance of the environment or context in which the goals are set includes everything from the availability and quality of resources, to relative buy-in by leadership and stake-holders.

➤ Companies evaluated their employees by comparing them with the "ideal" employee, thereby appraisal of traits only looks at what employees should be, not at what they should do.

➤ MBO would be counterproductive, when this approach is not properly set, agreed and managed by organizations. Self-centered employees might be prone to distort results, falsely representing achievement of targets that were set in a short-term and a narrow fashion.

➤ The use of MBO must be carefully aligned with the culture of the organization and employees ahould be involved in this process, which can be advantageous.

➤ "What gets measured gets done", a saying around MBO may lead to, the question:'Why measure performance? Different purposes require different measures' – is perhaps the most famous aphorism of performance measurement; therefore, to avoid potential problems SMART [Specific; Measurable; Achievable; Relevant; Time bound] and SMARTER [In some sectors (Healthcare, Finance etc.) many add ER to make SMARTER, The ER can have many meanings incluing E=End-minded R=Ritualistic[3] E=Energizing, Exciting and Ethical Goals or E=Evaluate or E=Ecological - consider 'whole' self; R=Reviewed and Resourced or R= Redo Goals or Recorded or R=Reasons and Reward] objectives need to be agreed upon in the true sense rather than set.

2.8   ARGUMENTS AGAINST MBO

W. Edwards Deming, one of the detractors of MBO, argued that a lack of understanding of systems commonly results in the misapplication of objectives.[9] Additionally, Deming stated that setting production targets will encourage resources to meet those targets through whatever means necessary, which usually results in poor quality.[10] Point 7 of Deming's key principles encourages managers to abandon objectives in favour of leadership because he felt that a leader with an understanding of systems was more likely to guide workers to an appropriate solution than the incentive of an objective. Deming also pointed out that Drucker warned managers that a systemic view was required and felt that Drucker's warning went largely unheeded by the practitioners of MBO.[11]

2.9 CONCLUDING REMARKS

"The Economist" remarked: "MBO is one of the rational school of management's successful products." MBO is a systematic and organized approach that allows management to focus on achievable goals and to attain the best possible results from available resources as tt aims to increase organizational performance by aligning goals and subordinate objectives throughout the organization. MBO includes ongoing tracking and feedback in the process to reach objectives and ideally, employees get strong input to identify their objectives, time lines for completion, etc. MBO has many features. It is a philosophy or a system, and not merely

---

[9] Deming, W. Edwards, "Out of the Crisis", The MIT Press, 1994, ISBN 0-262-54116-5

[10] Deming, W. Edwards, "Out of the Crisis", The MIT Press, 1994, ISBN 0-262-54116-5

[11] Drucker, Peter, "Management Tasks, Responsibilities, Practices", Harper & Row, 1973

technique. It emphasizes participative goal setting and clearly defines each individual responsibility in terms of results and focuses attention on what must be accomplished (goals) rather than on how it is to be accomplished. It converts objective needs into personal goals at every level in the organization and establishes standards or yardsticks (goals) as operation guides and also as basis of performance evaluation. It is a system intentionally directed toward effective and efficient attainment of organizational and personal goals. MBO process (or management by Objective cycle or key elements of management by Objectives or minimum equirements of management by objectives. There are four important and essential steps or elements in the management by Objectives process, namely: (a) setting objectives; (b) developind action plans; (c) Monitoring the progress/periodic review; (d) Performance appraisal.

MBO has many advantages. MBO programs continually emphasize what should be done in an organization to achieve organizational goals and its process secures employee commitment to attaining organizational goals. It involves employees in the whole process of goal setting and increasing employee empowerment increases employee job satisfaction and commitment, its frequent reviews and interactions between superiors and subordinates helps to maintain harmonious relationships within the enterprise and also solve many problems faced during the period. With MBO, came the concept of SMART and SMARTER goals.

MBO, however, is not free from disadvantages. MBO over-emphasizes the setting of goals over the working of a plan as a driver of outcomes. MBO underemphasizes the importance of the environment or context in which the goals are set. That context includes everything from the availability and quality of resources, to relative buy-in by leadership and stake-holders.

Management By Objectives (MBO) in Enterprises

Companies evaluated their employees by comparing them with the "ideal" employee. Trait appraisal only looks at what employees should be, not at what they should   do.
MBO did not address the importance of successfully responding to obstacles and constraints as essential to reaching a goal.

The use of MBO needs to be carefully aligned with the culture of the organization. While MBO is not as fashionable as it was before the 'empowerment' fad, it still has its place in management today. The key difference is that rather than 'set' objectives from a cascade process, objectives are discussed and agreed, based upon a more strategic picture being available to employees. By many researchers, engagement of employees in the objective setting process is seen as a strategic advantage.

Chapter 3

TOWARDS UNDERSTANDING 'MBO' PROCESS

3.1 INTRODUCTION

The process starts with good preparation including orientation to all members of the management team with an emphasis that active involvement in the 'MBO' program is an integral part of each manager's job. The next step is to communicate organization goals (including the chief executive directive) to subordinates at each level of organization hierarchy and review/discuss the superior's important job responsibilities, followed by the discussion and joint agreement on key effectiveness components of subordinate's job. Once understanding is built up regarding responsibilities and obligations of both superior and subordinates, next step is to jointly set objective, targets and performance criteria followed by interim progress review and finally evaluating performance and distribution rewards with a feedback to the process for further developed.

3.2 PETER DRUCKER'S FIVE-STEP PROCESS FOR 'MBO'

Peter Drucker outlined the five-step process for MBO, see Fig. 6.1. Each stage has particular challenges that need to be addressed for the whole system to work effectively. These steps are briefly discussed herein below:

Set or Review Organizational Objectives: MBO starts with clearly defined strategic organizational objectives as if the organization isn't clear where it's going, no one working there will be either. Corporate objectives determine the motive and mission of the business and may be explained by trying to answer the question 'what is our business'. Following out of the corporate objectives are the long and short-term strategic objectives. Accordingly, initially, organizations have to set corporate objectives. Goal-setting or objective setting is a multistage process. It starts with the examining of the current statte of affaires, level of efficiency, threats, and opportunities. Then the key result areas are identified, such as product markets, improved services, lowered costs, work simplification, employee motivation, profitability innovation and social responsibility. The performance of these areas is critical for organization in the sense that failure in these areas may result in failure of the organization. And this is why they are known as "key" result areas. Peter Drucker says, objectives are important in every area where performance and results directly affect the survival and prosperity of business.

Cascading Objectives Down to Employees: The organization needs to set clear goals and objectives to support the corporate mission, which then need to cascade down from one organizational level to the next until they reach everyone. To make MBO goal and objective setting more effective, Drucker used the SMART acronym to set goals that were attainable and to which people felt accountable. He said that goals and objectives must be: Specific; Measurable; Agreed (relating to the participative management principle); Realistic; and Time related. It is important that objectives to flow, or trickle, down through various stages of agreement as the only goal that is going to be met is one that is agreed on. For each objective, clear targets and performance standards need to be established. It's by using these that one can monitor progress throughout the organization. Also, these are important for communicating results, and for evaluating the suitability of the goals that have been set.

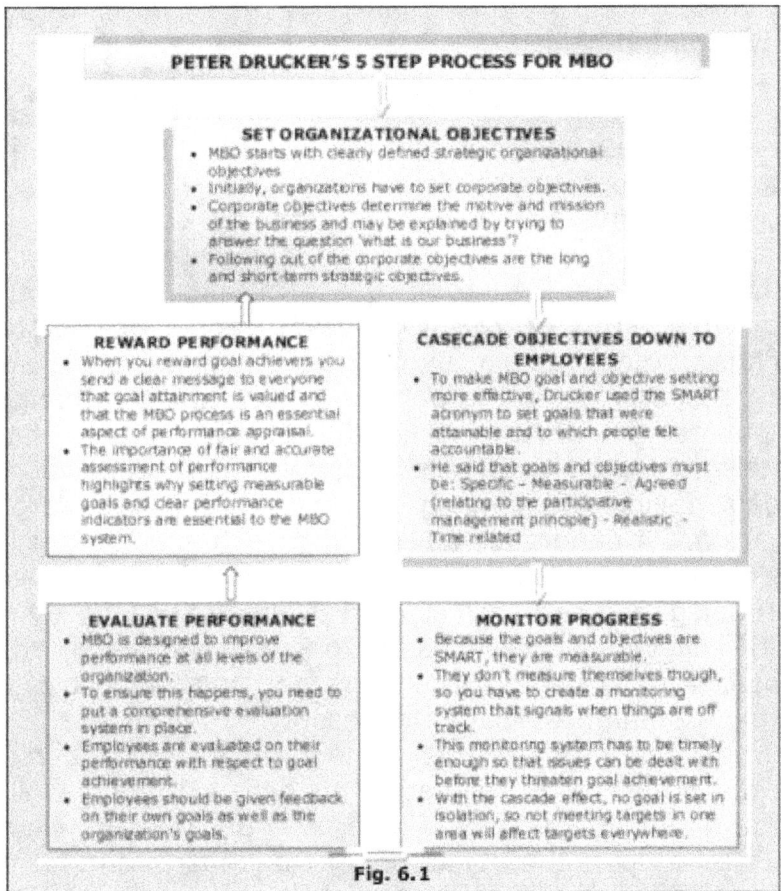

Fig. 6.1

Developing Action Planning Including Encourage Participation in Goal Setting: Planning allows the objectives to be transformed into reality. The objectives may be accomplished provided that the manager transforms them into certain action plans spelling out the different steps or functions to be performed and the specific time period within which these must be done. It requires assignment of specific responsibilities to different departments, division, and individuals and it also requires allocation of necessary resources needed to perform the assigned responsibilities. Time dimensions are also to be decided in order that targets are reached without any unwarranted delays.

In this respect, everyone needs to understand how their personal goals fit with the objectives of the organization. This is best done when goals and objectives are shared and discussed at each level, so that everyone understands "why" things are being done, and then sets their own goals to align with these objectives. This approach increases people's ownership of their objectives and by pushing decision-making and responsibility down through the organization, a manger motivate people to solve the problems they face intelligently and give them the information they need to adapt flexibly to changing circumstances. By and large, there are 4 general steps linked to each action plan: (i) selecting strategies that are suitable for the objectives; (ii) delegating responsibility for attaining the objectives; (iii) allocating resources for accomplishing the objectives; and (iv) Scheduling particular activities to attain optimum utilisation of resources. At this stage, a participative process is very important as: every person in the organization will set his or her own goals, which in turn support the overall objectives of the team, which in turn support the objectives of the department, which in turn support the objectives of the business unit, and which in turn support the objectives of the organization.

Performance review/Monitor Progress: After setting objectives and developing action plans, it is necessary to establish a proper monitoring system with a view to regularly keeping the activities. It is ensured that the deviations found, if any, are thoroughly discussed and immediate corrective actions are taken to set them right on the course. Such a regular monitoring and periodic review not only provide feedback which is essential for completion of work in time, but also motivates the managers accountable for performance. Because the goals and objectives are SMART, they are measurable. This monitoring system has to be timely enough so that issues can be dealt with before they threaten goal achievement. With the cascade effect, no goal is set in isolation, so not meeting targets in one area will affect targets everywhere. Regular performance review is among the primary functions of MBO and the main focus of the performance review is on: performance; improvement; future corrective action; and self-appraisal. Generally, periodic review and monitoring are done at departmental level.

Performance appraisal: This evaluates performance annually. The annual review or appraisal is comprehensive and is done at the organization level. The actual annual results are evaluated against the set objectives. Such assessment is also used for determining targets for next year, for modification in standards (goals) if needed, and for taking corrective actions in order to avoid deviations form predetermined objectives. MBO is designed to improve performance at all levels of the organization. To ensure this happens, you need to put a comprehensive evaluation system in place. As goals have been defined in a specific, measurable and time-based way, the evaluation aspect of MBO is relatively straightforward. Employees are evaluated on their performance with respect to goal achievement (allowing appropriately for changes in the environment.)

Reward Performance: All that is left to do is to tie goal achievement to reward, and perhaps compensation, and provide the appropriate feedback. Respective manager should send a clear message to everyone that goal attainment is valued and that the

MBO process is not just an exercise but an essential aspect of performance appraisal. The importance of fair and accurate assessment of performance highlights why setting measurable goals and clear performance indicators are essential to the MBO system. Employees should be given feedback on their own goals as well as the organization's goals.

3.3   ESSENTIAL ELEMENTS OF 'MBO' MODEL

There are six elements of 'MBO' Process which may be considered critical to the successful implementation of 'MBO'. The process is shown in Fig. 6.2.

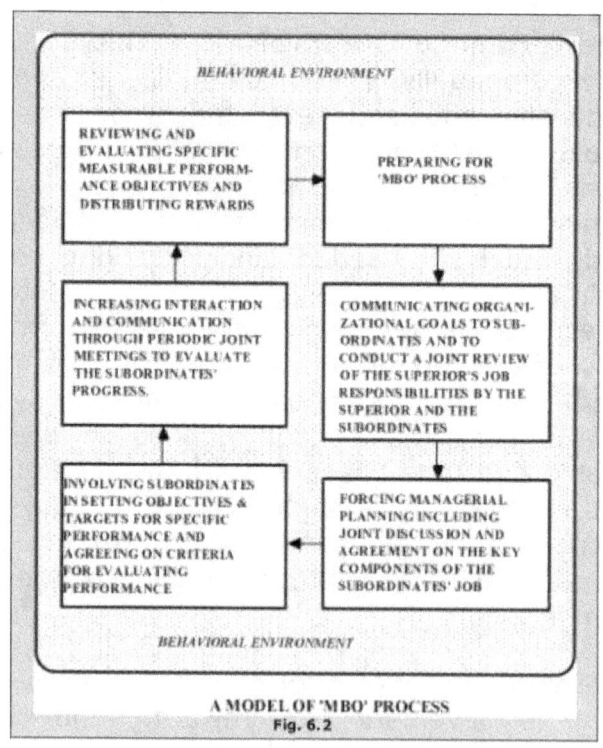

A MODEL OF 'MBO' PROCESS
Fig. 6.2

Chapter 4

THEORY, PRINCIPLES AND PROCESS FOR GOALS SETTING

4.1   INTRODUUCTION

The first empirical studies were performed by Cecil Alec Mace in 1935.[12] Edwin A. Locke began to examine goal setting in the mid-1960s and continued researching goal setting for thirty years. Locke derived the idea for goal-setting from Aristotle's form of final causality. Aristotle speculated that purpose can cause action; thus, Locke began researching the impact goals have on individual activity of its time performance. Goal setting theory was developed by Edwin A. Locke in the 1960s. His first article on goal setting theory was "Toward a Theory of Task Motivation and Incentives" which was published in 1968. It is considered an "open" theory, so as new discoveries are made it is modified. Studies have shown that specific and high goals lead to a higher level of performance than easy or general goals. There is a positive linear relationship between goal difficulty and task performance, as long as the individual: accepts the goal; has the ability to attain it; and does not have conflicting goals.

Goals are a form of motivation that set the standard for self-satisfaction with performance.[13] It has been said that "Goal setting capitalize on the human

------

[12] Cecil Alec Mace: The man who discovered goal-setting, by Paula Phillips Carsona; Kerry D. Carsona; Ronald B. Headya; International Journal of Public Administration, Volume 17, Issue 9 1994 , pp. 1679 - 1708
[13] Locke, Edwin; Gary Latham (2006), "New Directions in Goal-Setting Theory", *Association for Psychological Science* **15** (5): 265–268

brain's amazing powers: Our brains are problem-solving, goal-achieving machines." Accordingly, achieving the goal one has set for oneself is a measure of success, and being able to meet job challenges is a way one measures success in the workplace.

On a personal level, setting goals helps people work towards their own objectives—most commonly with financial or career-based goals. Goal setting involves establishing specific, measurable, achievable, realistic and time-targeted (SMART) goals. Work on the theory of goal-setting suggests that it's an effective tool for making progress by ensuring that participants in a group with a common goal are clearly aware of what is expected from them. Goal setting features as a major component of personal development literature. The researchers have found that goals that are deemed difficult to achieve and specific tend to increase performance more than goals that are not.[14] Setting goals affects outcomes in four ways:[15] (1) Choice: goals narrow attention and direct efforts to goal-relevant activities, and away from perceived undesirable and goal-irrelevant actions. (2) Effort: goals can lead to more effort; for example, if one typically produces 4 widgets an hour, and has the goal of producing 6, one may work more intensely towards the goal than one would otherwise. (3) Persistence: Someone becomes more prone to work through setbacks if pursuing a goal.

---

[14] Swezey, Robert W.; Meltzer, Zach L.; Salas, Jimmy M. (1994), "Some Issues Involved in Motivating Teams", in O'Neil, Tyler; Drillings, Holden L., *Motivation: health class research*, Lawrence Erlbaum Associates, p. 146, ISBN 0-8058-1287-3

[15] Latham, Gary P.; Budworth, Marie-Hélène (1492), "The Study of Work Motivation in the 20th Century", in Koppes, Laura L., *Historical Perspectives in Industrial and Organizational Psychology*, Lawrence Erlbaum Associates, p. 366,

(4) Cognition: Goals can lead individuals to develop and change their behavior.

4.2 DEVELOPMENTS IN GOAL SETTING THEORY

Goal Choice: According to Locke and Gary: self-efficacy, past performance and various other social factors influence goal setting[16]. Failure to meet previous goals often leads to setting lower (and more likely achievable) goals.

Learning Goals: According to Locke and Gary: there are times when having specific goals is not a best option; this is the case when the goal requires new skills or knowledge. "Tunnel vision" is a consequence of specific goals; if one is too focused on attaining a specific goal they ignore the need to learn new skills or acquire new information. In situations like this, the best option is to set a learning goal, when a learning goal is a generalized goal to achieve knowledge in a certain topic or field, but it can ultimately lead to better performance in specific goals related to the learning goals.[17] Locke and Latham attribute this response to metacognition, believing that "a learning goal facilitates or enhances metacognition, namely: planning; monitoring; and evaluating progress toward goal attainment".[18] This is necessary in environments with little or no guidance and structure. Although jobs typically have set goals, individual goals and achievement can benefit from metacognition.

---

[16] Locke, Edwin; Gary Latham (2006), "New Directions in Goal-Setting Theory", *Association for Psychological Science* **15** (5): 265–268

[17] Locke, Edwin; Gary Latham (2006), "New Directions in Goal-Setting Theory", *Association for Psychological Science* **15** (5): 265–268
[18] Locke, Edwin; Gary Latham (2006), "New Directions in Goal-Setting Theory", *Association for Psychological Science* **15** (5): 265–268

Framing: According to Locke and Gary: how goals are viewed influences performance. When one feels threatened and or intimidated by a high goal they perform poorer than those who view the goal as a challenge and the framing of a goal as a gain or a loss influences one's eventual performance.[19]

Affect: According to Locke and Gary: realization of goals has an effect on feelings of success and satisfaction, thereby achieving goals has a positive effect, and failing to meet goals has negative consequences, but the affect of goals is not exclusive to one realm as success in one's job can compensate for feelings of failure in one's personal life.[20]

Group Goals: According to Locke and Gary: the relationship between group goals and individual goals influences group performance; when goals are compatible there is a positive effect, but when goals are incompatible the effects can be detrimental to the group's performance. They found that there is another factor at work in groups, and that is the sharing factor; a positive correlation exists between sharing information within the group and group performance, but in the case of group goals, feedback needs to be related to the group, not individuals, in order for it to improve the group's performance.[21]

Goals and Traits: According to Locke and Gary: on a basic level the two types of goals are learning

---

[19] Locke, Edwin; Gary Latham (2006), "New Directions in Goal-Setting Theory", *Association for Psychological Science* **15** (5): 265–268

[20] Locke, Edwin; Gary Latham (2006), "New Directions in Goal-Setting Theory", *Association for Psychological Science* **15** (5): 265–268

[21] Locke, Edwin; Gary Latham (2006), "New Directions in Goal-Setting Theory", *Association for Psychological Science* **15** (5): 265–268

goals and performance goals. Each possesses different traits associated with the kind of goal that is selected.[22] These traits include: (a) learning goals; (b) tasks where skills and knowledge can be acquired; and (c) performance goals. They sussested to: avoid tasks where error and judgment are possible; and select tasks that are easy to accomplish and will make one appear successful. A more complex trait-mediation study is the one conducted by Lee, Sheldon, and Turban[23], which yielded the following results:

> "Amotivated Orientation" (low confidence in one's capabilities) is associated with goal-avoidance motivation, and generally associated with lower goals levels and lower performance

> "Control Orientation" (extrinsic motivation) is associated with both avoidance and approach goals. Approach goals are associated with higher goal levels and higher performance.

> "Autonomy Goals" (intrinsic motivation) leads to mastery goals, enhanced focus, and therefore enhanced performance.

Macro-level Goals: According to Locke and Gary: this is goal setting applied to the company as a whole as cooperative goals reduce the negative feelings that occur as a result of alliances and the formation of groups and the most common parties involved are the company and its suppliers. They found that the three motivators for macro-level goals are: self-efficacy;

---

[22] Locke, Edwin; Gary Latham (2006), "New Directions in Goal-Setting Theory", *Association for Psychological Science* **15** (5): 265–268
[23] Lee, Felissa; Kennon Sheldon; Daniel Turban (2003), "Personality and the goalstriving process: The influence of achievement goal patterns, goal level, and mental focus on performance and enjoyment", *Journal of Applied Psychology* **88** (2): 256–265

growth goals; and organizational vision.[24]

Goals and Subconscious Priming: According to Locke and Gary: the effects of subconscious priming and conscious goals are independent, although a conscious goal has a larger effect and the interaction effect is that priming can enhance the effects of difficult goals, but it has no effect on easy goals. They also found that there is also the situation in which priming and conscious goals conflict with one another, and in this situation the conscious goals have a greater effect on performance.[25]

4.3   DERIVING GOAL SETTING USING TEMPORAL MOTIVATION THEORY

Locke and Latham (2004) note that goal setting theory lacks "the issue of time perspective".[26] Taking this into consideration, Steel and Konig (2006) utilize their Temporal Motivation Theory (TMT) to account for goal setting's effects, and suggest new hypotheses regarding a couple of its moderators: goal difficulty and proximity. According to them, the effectiveness of goal setting can be explained by two aspects of TMT: the principle of diminishing returns; and temporal discounting, and to take advantage of these elements, similar to the expression "the sum of the parts can be greater than the whole", a division of a project into

---

[24] Locke, Edwin; Gary Latham (2006), "New Directions in Goal-Setting Theory", *Association for Psychological Science* **15** (5): 265–268

[25] Locke, Edwin; Gary Latham (2006), "New Directions in Goal-Setting Theory", *Association for Psychological Science* **15** (5): 265–268

[26] Locke, E.A., & Latham, G.P (2004), "What should we do about motivation theory? Six recommendations for the twenty-first century", *Academy of Management Review* **29**: 388–403

several, immediate, subgoals appears.[27]

4.4   LIMITATIONS OF GOAL SETTING THEORY

Goal-setting theory, however, has some limitations. For example, in an organization, a goal of a manager may not align with the goals of the organization as a whole. In such cases, the goals of an individual may come into direct conflict with the employing organization; and without aligning goals between the organization and the individual, performance may suffer. Also, for complex tasks, goal-setting may actually impair performance. In these situations, an individual may become preoccupied with meeting the goals, rather than performing tasks. Some researchers feel that one possible drawback of goal setting is that implicit learning may be inhibited. This is because goal setting may encourage simple focus on an outcome without openness to exploration, understanding or growth.

4.5   ESSENTIAL PRINCIPLES FOR SETTING OBJECTIVES

There are certain principles which are considered essential for setting objectives such as the following:

➢ Good coverage of the manager's job should be taken in account to avoid any loopholes or weaknesses.
➢ Both the manager and his superior should mutually discuss, determine and agree the objectives.
➢ Number of objectives must be limited and kept to a minimum, as far as possible.

[27] Steel, P. & Konig, C.J., P.; Konig, C. J. (2006), "Integrating Theories of Motivation", *Academy of Management Review* **31** (#): 889–913

➢ Objective must be stated in a simple and clear language that managers will understand without any difficulty.

➢ Objectives should be focused on job and not the personality.

➢ Objective should be set at higher level than the previous period, but must be attainable.

➢ Objectives set should be realistic and meaningful in terms of organizational goals and also important result expected from the manager.

➢ Objective set should be flexible to accommodate any modification if any change in conditions demands.

➢ Objective set should be appropriately rated (i.e. more weightage to be given to the most important objectives).

➢ Assessment of performance should be done by comparing results obtained with pre-determined objectives.

4.6   SELECTION OF OBJECTIVES

Performance objectives for the managers are set in the following stages:

a. Analysing the Manager's authority and responsibility, i.e. determining basic functional responsibility of the manager and writing down clear statements related thereto.

b. Comparing Goals with Manager's Job: (i.e. writing down statements explaining the nature of relationship of goals with the functions, and its importance).

c. Preparing Initial Definition of Objectives: (i.e. making a preliminary list of tentative objectives for the manager in a form which will set the basis for mutual discussion to finalise the objectives).

d. Determining the Unit of Measure: (i.e. deciding on the yardstick for measuring the performance e.g. number of customer or volume of sales for sale promotion, earning profit, etch).

e. Selecting Specific Targets: (i.e. the degree of achievement expected from the manager e.g. increase overall turnover by 10%, this 10% is the specific target).

f. Discussing with the Manager and Finalising Objectives: (i.e. final discussion and arriving at a joint agreement on final objectives for a specific period).

4.7 GUIDELINES FOR DEVELOPING GOALS/OBJECTIVES

Over the years many theorists and practitioners have suggested a number of useful guidelines for developing objectives. Some of the salient guidelines are as follows:

➤ Objective should be consistent with the specific resources that will be needed for carrying them out (i.e. funds, facilities or equipment, availability of manpower, etc.).

➤ Objective should be expressed clearly (without ambiguity) and in written statements containing three important elements, namely: a clear action, an end result, and a target date.

➤ Objectives should be verifiable (i.e. two or more different observers should agree on their achievements).

➤ Objective should be reasonable/attainable, yet challenging (i.e. standard should be reasonably high to keep motivation to the optimal level).

➤ Objectives should cover the key results area of an organizational unit or individuals.

➢ Objectives should specify 'what' and ,when' and not , why' or 'how'.
➢ The number of objectives should be manageable and kept to a minimum.
➢ Objectives should be co-ordinated with other units and managers of the organization.
➢ The achievement of objectives should be under the control/authority of responsible person or unit to avoid frustration.

For a successful installation of MBO Program, implementation of above guidelines will prove a positive inducement and a definite asset for the organization. William Kearney have also provided specific guideline on how to construct behaviourally anchored rating scales which should also be referred.[28]

4.13 GOAL SETTING IN BUSINESS

In business, goal setting encourages participants to put in substantial effort. According to some researchers, managers cannot constantly drive motivation, or keep track of an employee's work on a continuous basis, therefore, goals are an important tool for managers, since goals have the ability to function as a self-regulatory mechanism that acquires an employee a certain amount of guidance. Shalley, 1995[29] and Locke and Latham (2002)[30] have distilled following four

[28] Kearney, W. J.- *'Behaviorally Anchored Rating Scales - MBOis Missing Ingredient'*/ Personnel Journal, Jan. 1979, pp.20-25.

[29] Shalley, Christina E. (April 1995), "Effects of Coaction, Expected Evaluation, and Goal Setting on Creativity and Productivity", *Academy of Management Journal* **38** (2): 483–503.

[30] Latham, G.; Locke, Edwin A. (2002), "Building a Practically Useful Theory of Goal Setting and Task Motivation", *The American Psychologist* **57**

mechanisms through which goal setting can affect individual performance:

1. Goals focus attention toward goal-relevant activities and away from goal-irrelevant activities.
2. Goals serve as an energizer: Higher goals induce greater effort, while low goals induce lesser effort.
3. Goals affect persistence; constraints with regard to resources affect work pace.
4. Goals activate cognitive knowledge and strategies that help employees cope with the situation at hand.

4.9   RELATIONSHIP OF GOAL–PERFORMANCE

Locke et al. (1981) examined the behavioral effects of goal-setting, concluding that 90% of laboratory and field studies involving specific and challenging goals led to higher performance than did easy or no goals.[31] While some managers believe it is sufficient to urge employees to 'do their best,' Locke and Latham have a contradicting view on this. Some authors state that people who are told to 'do their best' don't. 'Doing your best' has no external referent, which makes it useless in eliciting specific behavior. To elicit some specific form of behavior from others, it is important that this person has a clear view of what is expected from him/her. A goal is thereby of vital importance because it facilitates an individual in focusing their efforts in a specified direction. In other words, goals canalize behavior.[32] However, when goals are established at a management level and thereafter

---

(9): 705–17.

[31] Locke, Edwin A.; Shaw, Karyll N.; Saari, Lise M..; Latham, Gary P. (1981),"Goal Setting and Task Performance: 1969=1980), *Psychological Bulletin* (American Psychological Association) **90** (1): 125–152,

[32] Cummings & Worley p. 368.

solely laid down, employee motivation with regard to achieving these goals is rather suppressed.[33] To increase motivation, employees not only must be allowed to participate in the goal setting process, but the goals must be challenging as well.[34]

4.10 REALTIONSHIP OF EMPLOYEE MOTIVATION WITH GOAL SETTING

Bandura found that the more employees are motivated, the more they are stimulated and interested in accepting goals and these success factors are interdependent. For example, the expected outcomes of goals are positively influenced when employees are involved in the goal setting process; and not ot only does participation increase commitment in attaining the goals that are set, participation influences but also self-efficacy. Also, to this feedback is necessary to monitor one's progress. When this is left aside, an employee might think he/she is not making enough progress and thinking can reduce self-efficacy and thereby harm the performance outcomes in the long run.[35] Goal-commitment, the most influential moderator, becomes especially important when dealing with difficult or complex goals. If people lack commitment to goals, they lack motivation to reach them. To commit to a goal, one must believe in its importance or significance by considering the following:

Attainability: individuals must also believe that they can attain, or at least partially reach, a defined goal. If they think no chance exists of reaching a goal,

---

[33] Locke & Latham, 2002 p. 705.

[34] Cummings & Worley p. 369.

[35] Bandura, A. (March 1993), "Perceived Self-Efficacy in Cognitive Development and Functioning", *Educational Psychologist* **28** (2): 119–20.

they may not even try.

> **Self-efficacy:** Goal-setting theory might define "self-efficacy" as an impression that one has the capability of performing in a certain manner or of attaining certain goals. Or one could define "self-efficacy" as a belief that one has the capabilities to execute the courses of actions required to manage prospective situations. Unlike efficacy (defined as the power to produce an effect — in essence, competence), self-efficacy consists of the belief (whether or not accurate) that one has the power to produce that effect. For example, a person with high self-efficacy may engage in a more health-related activity when an illness occurs, whereas a person with low self efficacy may succumb to feelings of hopelessness. Compare David Sue, Derald Wing Sue, Stanley Sue, *Understanding Abnormal Behavior*, 8th edition, p. 214. — Note the distinction between self-esteem and self-efficacy. Self-esteem in this context relates to a person's sense of self-worth, whereas self-efficacy relates to a person's perception of their ability to reach a goal. For example, take the case of an incompetent rock-climber. Though probably afflicted with poor self-efficacy in regard to rock climbing, this hypothetical person could retain their self-esteem unaffected — most people don't invest much of their self-esteem in this activity. Accordingly, the higher someone's self-efficacy regarding a certain task, the more likely they will set higher goals, and the more persistence they will show in achieving them.

4.11 IMPACT OF FEEDBACK ON GOAL SETTING

According to some researchers, keeping track of performance to allow employees to see how effective they have been in attaining the goals in of paramount importance as without proper feedback channels it is impossible to adapt or adjust to the required behavior, therefore, goal setting and feedback go hand in hand.[36] Without feedback, goal setting is unlikely to work. Providing feedback on short-term objectives, helps to sustain motivation and commitment to a goal. Besides, feedback should be provided on the strategies followed to achieve the goals and the final outcomes achieved as well. Feedback on strategies to obtain goal is very important, especially for complex work, because challenging goals put focus on outcomes rather than on performance strategies, so they impair performance. Proper feedback is also very essential, and the following hints may help for providing a good feedback:

> Focus on behaviours and strategies.

> Use constructive and positive language.

> Create a positive context for feedback.

> Make feedback a two-way communication process.

> Tailor feedback to the needs of the individual worker.

Advances in technology can facilitate providing feedback. For example, Systems analysts have designed computer programs that track goals for numerous members of an organization and such computer systems may maintain every employee's goals, as well as their deadlines, whilst separate methods may check the employee's progress on a regular basis, and other

---

[36] Skinner, Natalie; Roche, Ann M.; O'Connor, John; Pollard, Yvette; Todd, Chelsea, Inders. Edu. Au "Goal setting", *Workforce Development 'TIPS' Theory Into Practice Strategies*, Alcohol Education and Rehabilitation Foundation Ltd (AER) 2005, pp. 8–9.

systems may require perceived slackers to explain how they intend to improve.

4.12 GOAL SETTING PROCESS

Whilst goal setting, it is important that the goals are well thought out. To ensure that use SMART or SMARTER goal setting process. SMART are goals that are:

M – Measurable; **A** - Achievable (yet challenging); **S** – Specific; and **T** - Time-targetted;

SMARTER are goals that are: **M** – Measurable; **A** - Achievable (yet challenging); **S** – Specific; **T** - Time-targetted; **E** – Energizing; and **R** - Relevant

The following procedure should be adopted:

➤ Write down the goals: Begin by generating a list of potential goals as by writing down goals gives them more force and also may make them tangible.

➤ Ensure that goals are well thought out.

➤ Design and use an appropriate goal setting worksheet.

➤ Determine a procedure to measre goal achievement.

➤ Establish the deadline for achieving each goal. When setting deadlines, consider:
  o Priorities – which goals are most important?
  o Prerequisites – do any goals require another goal to be accomplished first?
  o Reality – what organizational, unit, or individual constraints exist in accomplishing this goal?
  o Measures – does the timing of any of the

measures affect the deadline (e.g., a half-yearly survey)?

- o Make an entry in the goal setting worksheet.

➢ Identify any obstacle(s) in achieving the goal. Remember when the person has many goals, they will likely experience, conflict in the form of these goals competing for their time and attention. Therefore, it is important to consider all of these potential obstacles and make enteries of the most important obstacles in the Goal Setting Worksheet.

➢ Identify how to overcome obstacles. Once you have identified and listed the obstacles that may prevent you from achieving the goals, create a plan to address these obstacles and the enter in the goal setting worksheet, how the obstacle will be overcome.

➢ Review the list to ensure that all the goals are reasonable.

➢ Monitor progress and continue to set goals.

A proposed worksheet is shown in Fig. 6.3.

PROPOSED GOAL SETTING WORKSHEET

Name: .... Date: ....

Goal No.	Goal Description	Deadline	Potential Obstacles	Ways to Overcome Obstacles	Measure Success	Remarks
1						
2						
3						
4						
5						
6						
7						
8						
9						
10						

Fig. 6.3

We must remember that the process of setting goals is a never-ending one – it changes as our needs change and also effective goal setting is one of the most important habits we can develop as it is the core skill for achieving success. Accordingly, we we must take necessary steps and make our every move by placing all our effort in the right areas. We shouls follow our intuition, our inner guidance and it will lead us to take the right action every time. If we will make a commitment to follow our passion without hesitation until it becomes our reality, the chances for failure is very slim, in fact it is guaranteed that we will never fail.

Chapter 5

DEVELOPMENT OF ORGANIZATIONAL GOALS AND OBJECTIVES

5.1   INTRODUCTION

Organizational or management objectives give purpose and meaning of the organization and stem from the aim, mission and goals of the organization. Aim of an organization refers to the ends towards which activities are directed. Mission of an organization is the ultimate aim of the enterprise (i.e. its reason for existence). Goals are statements of aim in qualitative term directed towards the mission. Objectives are verifiable statements of aim directed towards the goals (i.e. clear statements of results to be achieved). the connection between aim (at the top) to objectives (at the bottom) form the objection hierarchy, which must be understood by all members of the organization, particularly when MBO approach to management is implemented in the organization. This requisite is stresses by Abran McGlow in these words: "It seems to me that in an enterprise, if everybody concerned is absolutely clear about the goals and directives and far purposes of the organization, practically all other questions then become simple technical questions of fitting means to the end."

According to Heinz Weihrick, the mission, goals and objectives should be integrated from top to bottom, starting from organization mission at the top moving downward through organizational goals, organizational objectives, department objectives, section objectives, group objective and ending at the bottom with individual performance objectives (written detailed statements). He further explains that in the development of objective, to achieve horizontal integration is also important as a well articulated objectives hierarchy must include both vertical and horizontal integration.[37]

5.2 MANAGEMENT OBJECTIVES

Main object of management is to secure maximum prosperity for both the employers and the employees. In organizations maximum prosperity for the employers may mean a state of optimal level of productivity and profits, whilst for the employees it may mean the development of each employee to his highest level of efficiency (i.e. maximum output) through training and development. In other words the determination of management objectives is concerned with establishing targets at all level of the organization hierarchy. For example, for the employers, objectives should measure performance in terms of contribution to profits, innovation or other significant goals and for the managers, objectives should be such that they can be understood by them, and they are attainable within the authority vested in them by the top management. By and large, management objectives are determined by the Board of Directors/Top Management of the respective enterprise, see Fig 6.3a.

---

[37] Weihrich, Heinz A.- ' Heirarchy and Network of Atoms: Getting More out of MBO/ Management Review, Jan. 1982.

FACTORS INFLUENCING THE FORMULATION OF THE
CORPORATION MISSION AND OBJECTIVES

Fig. 6.3a

5.3   PERFORMANCE OBJECTIVES

Performance objectives are statements describing the conditions of the job environment including measures to determine the extent to which the objectives are to be achieved. For example, 'Loss due to rejected item will not be more than 2% of the total production'. For deciding performance objectives, some thought should be given to the relationship between the enterprise's goals, the manager, and the authority vested in the manager. Some of the concepts in this respect include: saving costs, optimizing productivity, sales and profitability of the enterprise etc.

Generally, there is a hierarchy of performance objectives as some of them are important and carry more weightage, whilst others are less important and carry low weightage, see Fig. 6.4. A rating of performance objectives are fixed to provide suitable coverage of managers responsibilities. Therefore, basic idea of performance objectives is to provide a systematic method of measurement to indicate how well or how poorly each manager is performing. For example, if a manager has performed very well in important objective but not too well in objectives having a low value, his assessment for overall performance will be considered good. Satisfactory achievement of performance objectives provides satisfaction to both the manager as well as his superior. To the manager in the form of increased motivation and to his superior because he does not want uncertainty about performance level of his subordinates.

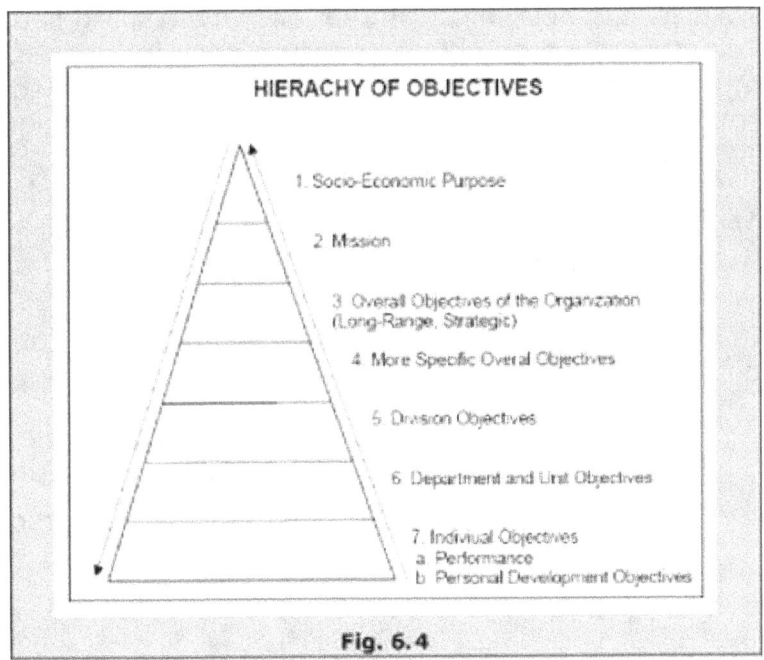

Fig. 6.4

Management By Objectives (MBO) in Enterprises

Performance objectives may have many categories, but most useful and meaningful types include: (i) direct performance objectives, and (ii) indirect performance objectives. Brief description of each is given below:

Direct Performance Objectives: Objectives pertaining to tasks in which performance can be measured in terms of results directly and quantitatively, such as: increase in production/turnover, reduction in cost, improvement in sales and/or profitability etc.

Indirect Performance Objectives: Objectives pertaining to the characteristics of the manager himself (i.e. related to technical/administrative skills, personal traits and behavior etc.) and include his leadership qualities, his motivation, his attitude, his stamina, his health, etc. These characteristics are not so easily measurable in abstract term, yet are important in setting of objectives for complete measurement for managers performance. This type of objectives are graded in terms of importance (i.e. rating system) with assigned weightage in accordance with value rather than measuring in terms of results. For measuring indirect objectives, reference should be made to the principles used for performance appraisal.

Some examples of indirect objectives about managerial characteristics are as follows:

- Integrity, reliability, and leadership ability.
- Initiative, intelligence and tactfulness.
- Technical skills, conceptual skills, interpersonal skills diagnostic skills and analytic skills.

> ➢ Ability to organize, ability to plan, ability to develop and motivate staff and ability to make decisions.
> ➢ Administrative ability, resourcefulness and judgement.
> ➢ Spirit of co-operation, physical health and stamina.

5.4   CONCLUDING REMARKS

In practice, there are some problems in defining professional and non-professional objectives and standards of performance in abstract terms. Certainly if an MBO scheme is to be implemented the establishing the aims and objectives of the enterprise/institution are necessary, therefore, agreement among staff on this score will not always be easy to achieve. There may be reluctance to commit oneself to any statement of aims beyond a very general one, as if we assume that some agreement can be reached on the educational, economic, business, commercial, aims and objectives of the organization, thereby requiring strategic and tactical planning in order to achieve them. Strategic planning would be concerned with long-term changes, a limited number of high priority objectives, that could be translatable into tactical plans having a more immediate effect on the organization. These tactical or action plans would affect the institution`s work over the near-future, say, over two years. Departmental objectives would now be identified. The question of measurement of departmental objectives arises: some can be measured; others cannot [especially true in educational contexts]. Succinctly, the position may be expressed that those who argue only quantifiable objectives are relevant fail to understand that they may be closely related to unquantifiable objectives of equal or greater importance.

Chapter 6

PERFORMANCE APPRAISAL AND FEEDBACK

6.1   INTRODUCTION

MBO and its inherent appraisal systems (performance reviews and staff development) depend on accurate and meaningful job-descriptions being written, which are often perfunctory documents giving the impression of being somewhat hastily put together. Such job-desriptions will not do at all in the service of a thoroughgoing system of management by objectives, therefore, those job descriptions that are apt and tailored for the post, are essential. Creating such documents demandss much work and time must be put aside for their accomplishment. Such deocument, by and large are known by a candidate for a post before being invited for interview.

By means of performance appraisal, the management process is evaluated, i.e. how well (or otherwise) the enterprise is doing and the individual`s contribution to these goals and objectives is assessed. Without the setting of objectives to offer standards to judge by, it is obvious that performance dialogues can have little meaning. Ideally, both partners (manager and subordinate) in the exercise should enjoy the situation once it has been established that an impartial stance has been taken up by the manager. Also by means of these performance appraisal, accountability accountability of both resources and results is clarified. Performance appraisal is an active process where both partners in the transaction experience a meting of minds. To end this section, a quote from Paul Mali is appropriate: "...a performance appraisal program that uses MBO is both a `rating` device for evaluating individual performance and a `managing` procedure to ensure the processes of management".

6.2   VERIFIABLE MEASURES

The researchers have found that an objective appraisal with verifiable measures is better than subjective evaluation by perceptions, as verifiable measures are quantitative or descriptive. Using numbers is not the only objective way to measure., but it requires the thinking of quantitative measures only is limiting and can result in measuring what is easily quantifiable but not what is most important. Descriptive measures are complementary to quantitative ones when numbers don't make sense, buut according to Drucker: "These measurements need not to be rigidly quantitative; nor need they be exact, but they have to be clear, simple, and rational." Measuring performance, however, can help drive desired business results and the key to successful performance measurement is to collect only those performance measures that can or will actually be used.

6.3   RESULT-ORIENTED PERFORMANCE

Activity-oriented measurements focus on activity, behavior, or actions which are means, not ends as it generates more activity, because what gets measured gets done., aim at the results to attain objectives, not the activity or competency! Competencies define what skills, knowledge and experience an individual needs in order to produce results. Therefore, having a skill and using it successfully, are two very different things. According to Weihrich: "In its early application, MBO overcame some of the problems of traditional appraisals that emphasized personality traits. In MBO appraisal, on the other hand, the focus is on results. Performance is evaluated against verifiable objectives, rather than purely subjective judgments by the superior. Moreover, in MBO the attention is on contributions individuals make to the broader organizational aims."[38]

6.4   SELF-CONTROL

The results of performance measurement should be the means of self-control, not a tool of control from above, and should go directly to the one who is evaluated instead of to his or her manager. A researcher has well said: "The greatest advantage of management by objectives is perhaps that it makes it possible for a manager to control his own performance. Self-control means stronger motivation: a desire to do the best rather than just enough to get by. It means higher performance goals and broader vision."

6.5   PERFORMANCE FEEDBACK

A manager will make contributions to enterprises only if he/she is effective and efficient. For a manager to know his objectives is for him/her to do the right things, but how well does he/she do the things right? A researcher remarked: "To be able to control his own performance, a manager needs to know more than what his/her goals are. Therefore, attaining objectives is a progress of improvement, as a researcher remarked: "A critical enabler in achieving desired performance goals is the ability to measure performance." (Harbour) as Drucker remarked: "You can't improve what you

---

[38] Weihrich, Heinz A.- ' Heirarchy and Network of Atoms: Getting More out of MBO/ Management Review, Jan. 1982.

can't (or don't) measure, The manager must be able to measure his/her performance and results against the goal." Accordingly, an effective performance appraisal system relies on objective measures and results instead of subjective perceptions of manager, stresses on self-control measurement but control from above, and provides continuous and immediate feedback of performance information.

6.6   CONTINUOUS FEEDBACK

Performance feedback needs to be continuous and immediate so that attaining objectives is a progress of improvement and actions to improve never come to an end. According to Drucker: "Each manager should have the information he/she needs to measure his/her own performance and should receive it soon enough to make any changes necessary for the desired results." Accodingly, the goal of any performance measurement system is to provide the right people with the right performance-related information at the right time. Equipped with this information, the enterprise can make on-the-spot adjustments in work assignments to ensure customers are receiving the highest level of service possible. A researcher has found that, one highly successful service enterprise, for example, has developed a real-time computer-based performance system that can collect and distribute a number of performance measures, depicting how rapidly the company is responding to various customer requests.

Chapter 7

EVLOLUTION OF MBO: FROM MBO TO BALANCED SCORECARD

7.1   INTRODUCTION

MBO was first outlined by Peter Drucker in 1954. MBO is a systematic and organised approach that allows management to focus on achievable goals and to attain the best possible results from available resources, whilst aiming to increase organisational performance by aligning goals and subordinate objectives throughout the organization; and it includes ongoing tracking and feedback in the process to reach objectives.

7.2 TIMELINE OF EVOLUTION OF MANAGEMENT BY OBJECTIVES

A researcher, Jan Elembemavag arrived at some major management milestones along with the most prominent proponents by pointing out that the timeline is only approximate. See Fig. 6.5.

If we start from the beginning of the timeline, it is important to note that when Drucker presented Management By Objectives (MBO), a system that was originally conceived at DuPont and General Motors in the early twentieth century under the name "MBO and self-control", managers were dictated people what to do in detail, but Drucker turned it around and advocated that if people were told what was expected (an objective) they would themselves find out *how to* achieve the goal, thereby MBO was taken as a revolutionary idea.

In early 1960s, Deming was more concerned with how things were done and how to ensure total customer satisfaction (quality) and he did not approve of MBO in the extreme case, i.e. that anything works as long as you reach the goal and in that respect Drucker MBO was only the first step on the path towards better management practices. Japanese industry was at the forefront in accepting Deming viewpoint that 'how things were done did matter for both costs and quality. When Deming published his book *Out of the Crisis* in the early 1980s, it was then when US industry finally appreciated the Deming viewpoint. But around same time there were more problems for managers due to increasing competition as the world economy stagnated and the increasing automation-, sales and marketing-, product development and overhead costs in general lead to the development of Strategic Management. Porter viewpoint further emphasized the need for cost management approaches that took the process view into account and this opened the way for Activity-Based Costing.

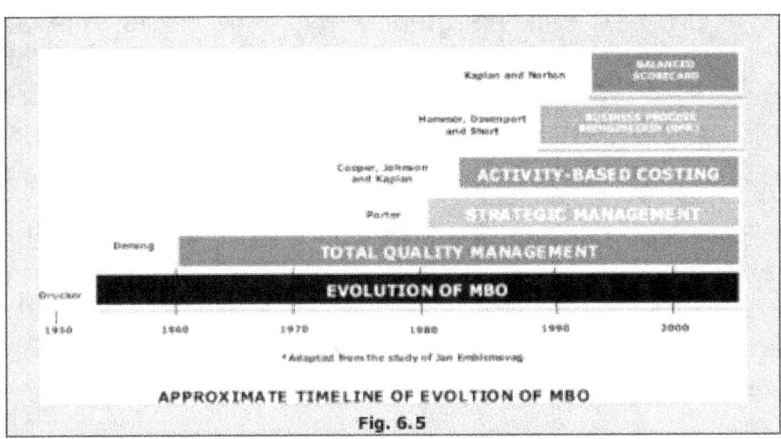

APPROXIMATE TIMELINE OF EVOLTION OF MBO

Fig. 6.5

Management By Objectives (MBO) in Enterprises

Whilst Strategic Management aided organizations in identifying, developing and defending their Sustainable Competitive Advantage (SCA), ABC was seen as the art of simplicity versus reliability and a more clever way to assign cost, but many practitioners do not link ABC to Total Quality Management (TQM) and MBO, links that are crucial in order to realize the highest potential of ABC. About importance these vital links, Jan Elembemavag has highlighted this aspect as follows:

> "ABC needs TQM to avoid the business as usual syndrome - to ensure that continuous improvement takes place. ABC is after all mostly an attention directing tool and not a miracle cure.

> ABC needs MBO to ensure that the management process works, because even the results from a world class system are useless unless they are managed properly.

> TQM needs ABC to establish the vital link between quality and costs, because as Vice-Chairman of Chrysler Robert Lutz said "too much quality can ruin you".

> MBO needs ABC to ensure that the management process can be guided by timely and relevant information and not by too aggregated, too late and too distorted information that characterizes most management systems."

ABC was useful to identify areas of improvement and critical success factors followed by yet another development, i.e. Business Process Reengineering (BPR), which realigns processes and refocuses the organization towards its purpose. PBR was found as a complementary aspect to TQM.

Arouund mid 1990s, Kaplan and Norton have shown that organizations can be managed well and kept focused on their strategies with a small set of metrics as long as they are chosen wisely. Hence, the notion of a Balanced Scorecard was born. While, the management by objectives (MBO) approach is perhaps one of the earliest systematic approaches to working with goals and objectives, the balanced scorecard is aimed to make key improvements on a simple MBO system, particularly by more clearly tying goals and objectives to vision, mission, and strategy, and branching out beyond purely financial goals and objectives. The MBO evolved over the years.

7.3   FIFTY (50) YEARS APPRAISAL OF MBO

Grigorios Kyriakopoulos School of Electrical and Computer Engineering of the National Technical University of Athens (NTUA), Greece has conducted a review study on the evolution of half a century of MBO. The relevant research is spanning over the last five decades and an approach to position representative common characteristics of this wide spectrum of studies, was implemented through their grouping into 15 main areas of application. The presented studies were analyzed, revealing the favourable areas of application by using the MBO approach. Among 82 literature survey, it was found that the main area of MBO application was in the medical sector. The four main medical subgroupings of healthcare, that is, healthcare, nursing, hospital management and hospital pharmacy account for 40% of the total references. The study lso denoted determining factors of potential MBO malfunction, such as: the observing distortion between MBO introductory structure and its function in real business environments, which were proved detrimental to their operation. Some highlights of this study are given herein below.

Operational strategy, was encouraged by Drucker (1954) in his theory of management by objectives (MBO). Operational level strategies are informed by business level strategies which, in turn, are informed by corporate level strategies. The introduction of strategic management to the businesses market originated in the 1950s and 1960s. Among the numerous early contributors to the relevant literature, the most influential and notable pioneers of strategic management were Chandler (1962), Selznick 1957), Ansoff (1965) and Drucker (1954). The idea of matching the organization's internal factors with external environmental circumstances was introduced by Selznick (1957).

According to Chandler (1962) the importance of coordinating the various aspects of management under one all-encompassing strategy was pointed out. Since then, the various functions of management were separate, having little overall coordination or strategy. The determining mechanism of Chandler's (1962) theory was the occurring interactions between functions or between departments, whilst these interactions were typically handled by a boundary position (by one or two managers) that relayed information back and forth between two departments. Chandler also stressed the significance of taking a long-term perspective when looking to the future (Chandler, 1962). This fundamental idea was developed into the well known Strengths-Weaknesses-Opportunities-Threads (SWOT) analysis introduced by Learned, Andrews, and his colleagues at the Harvard Business School General Management Group.

Ansoff's (1965): Work is built on Chandler's (1962) approach by adding a range of strategic concepts and inventing a whole new vocabulary. He developed a strategy grid that compared the marketing types, such as: market penetration; market development, product development, diversification; and horizontal and vertical integration.

Ansoff (1965): In the classic Corporate Strategy, published in 1965, developed the gap analysis, in which the key-factor is the understanding the gap existence between where we are currently and where we would like to be. Based on gapanalysis Ansoff (1965) consequently developed what he called "gap reducing actions".

Reif and Bassford (1973): MBO in the current (1970s) business environment. This study describes the concept and its emphasis on results and on human behaviour and motivation. The system has the four basic components, namely: (a) setting objectives; (b) developing action plans; (c) conducting periodic reviews; and (4) appraising annual performance.

McConkey (1973) : MBO in the current (1970s) business environment. This study states that any significant validation of MBO effectiveness has yet (1970s) to be done. The study is also serving as a preliminary evaluation for MBO, tracing the important steps in the development of the system and making some general appraisals on the extent to which it has been adopted. Moreover, some of the primary changes, which MBO created in the management process, are discussed, as well as some of the reasons why MBO has failed in certain situations. Finally, the author considers the future of MBO, according to the present indicators of its future placement in management systems.

Anonymous (1974): MBO in the current (1970s) business environment. This purpose of this study is to ensure the MBO by using the managerial grid.

Fri (1974): MBO and politics This study examines the ways of managing the government for results, using the MBO perspective.

Odiorne (1974): MBO and politics, This study correlates the politics of implementing the MBO theory.

Hand and Hollingsworth (1975): MBO in hospital management. The purpose of this study is to prescribe a remedy utilizing MBO, in order to elucidate the phenomenon of high employee turnover rates in hospitals, which detract from the quality of patient care and sub optimize financial resources.

Hives (1975): MBO in the current (1970s) business environment: MBO characteristic is that it rarely seems able to sustain the promise of its initial impact because it is essentially bosses' movements rather than popular movements. The MBO ideology does, however, come close to that of a genuine social movement if only it is interpreted and applied correctly. The convergence of MBO and the Organisation Development movement promises that together they will be seen as an acceptable response to the changing expectations and values of the participants in the currently large, augmenting and complex businesses.

William (1975): Differentiating MBO and appraisal systems. This study focuses on differentiating MBO and appraisal systems, in a contingency viewpoint within the business environment.

Futrell et al. (1977): MBO in hospital products' sales management. The study reports the results of a MBO evaluation program for over 200 salesmen in a hospital products company. The main favourable and unfavourable effects of the MBO program were also discovered.

Sims (1977): MBO in industrial sales management. This study focuses on the area of sales management, as a key-point which can benefit from the MBO procedure. The unique characteristics and activities of salesmen and sales managers demand a flexible tool of evaluation are also presented. The study's objectives are: the examination of some specific problems and needs of industrial sales management, the outline of suggested MBO procedures for industrial sales management, and a discussion on how MBO can operationally deal with the problems and needs of industrial sales management.

Odiorne (1978): MBO in the current (1970s) business environment: The study presents a backward glance of the MBO theory in the current business environment.

Cassidy (1979): MBO structural analysis; MBO as a theory of life's goodness. According to this study, MBO is viewed as a theory of life's goodness, especially within the businesses' environment.

Dirsmith and Jablonsky (1979): MBO as a governmental means for managing agencies and programs. This study aims at MBO evaluation as a management technique and as a political strategy, using concepts developed in the organizational theory, general systems theory, planning and control, and political science literatures. The study's results that MBO falls short of its mark and that it has been primarily used as a political strategy for controlling and directing controversy.

Ford (1979): MBO in the current (1970s) business environment. The present study is chronologically placed with the critical third decade of MBO introduction. During this period, MBO is generally valued as a not successful theory with questionable usefulness, because of what appears to be an inherent conceptual problem. This severe critical standpoint of MBO has also stated that if this theory could leave to us any kind of legacy, it will be to serve as a guideline to the mistakes new concepts should avoid.

McConkie (1979): MBO structural analysis; Clarification of the goal setting and appraisal processes in MBO. The notions of "goal setting" and "performance appraisal" have assumed many different shapes and purposes within the MBO concept. The MBO concept clarification is materialized in this review study through various writings of leading MBO experts' examination. Moreover, the study extracts those elements common to their respective definitions of goal setting and performance appraisal, and joins them into a single definition of MBO.

Bell (1980): MBO in nursing. In this study, MBO is explained and its advantages for nursing management discussed, according to its stimulating growth and measuring performance in an organization. The study reveals the way of the system implementation and success. Additionally, two examples of MBO in nursing are given, namely staff evaluation and patient care planning.

Cheetham (1980): MBO application within a building contracting company. The present study presents the philosophies and techniques that the MBO technique incorporates, with reference to a case study development within a building contracting company.

Fischer and McLaughlin (1980): MBO and Research and Development (R&D) in organizations. MBO is successfully addresses both job design and motivational incentives for the majority of organizations' efforts towards increasing productivity. The study examines the dynamic of both MBO and R&D setting, regarding the overall system's desirability. Alternatively, the approach to MBO stresses the non-evaluative contributions an MBO system can make to the researcher. The results of applying this alternative approach to simulated MBO and R&D setting results in a substantial increase in productivity and the maintenance of social harmony within the group.

Garrison and Raynes (1980): MBO in the healthcare sector. This study denotes the challenge of the burgeoning complexity of administering mental health programs calls for increasingly sophisticated management strategies. Moreover, MBO is considered an administrative tool that may assist mental health managers in meeting administrative needs, as well as service demands in a more efficient fashion. Additionally, the study describes the results of a pilot MBO project applied to an outpatient service in a community mental health centre.

Taylor (1980): MBO in the healthcare sector. The scope of the present study originates from management-coordinated efforts of a network of organizational members and health professionals, in order to effective health protection and materialization at the workplace. Moreover, the application of a specific MBO program to preventive health care in an industrial corporation is discussed.

Wallace (1980): MBO in nursing. The study provides various aspects of consultation and MBO.

Cornillon et al. (1981): MBO in hospital

management. Hospital on objectives is an enormous and dangerous objective, therefore, it should be for a good reason and be linked with deep-going causes. The authors ask themselves about the evolution of the French administrative environment, which is the factor causing a great number of obstacles, in particular, of the planning negotiated between the State and the public enterprises. The study states that governing by objectives is a technique of management; but in the hospital there is no concentration of power in the hands of one person. Thus, the study attempts to identify who are the real prime movers – "those persons who get things done" – both internally and externally.

Covaleski and Dirsmith (1981): MBO in hospital management. In this study an attempt to implement the management of two hospitals, using the MBO system as a means of improving organizational planning and control. The study concluded that, as a goal-directed form of management technology, MBO may lead to dysfunctional decision making at the institutional level within organizations, especially those facing complex, dynamic environments. Nevertheless, in case that MBO is viewed as a philosophy of management administered at the sub-unit level, it may serve as a catalytic agent for encouraging decentralized decision making and performance evaluation.

Deegan 2 (1981): MBO in hospital management. The study handles the functionality and appropriateness of MBO in hospital management.

Kondrasuk (1981): MBO in employee productivity and job satisfaction. MBO system efficacy remains questionable at the era of the study's publication. Therefore, the present study analyzes numerous studies for the effects of MBO on employee productivity and job satisfaction. Research support for MBO was found to be inversely related to the degree of research design sophistication. Moreover, it appears a contingency approach to MBO is more appropriate than a definitive affirmation or rejection of MBO effectiveness.

Alberts (1982): MBO structural analysis. MBO is considered as a participative management system, leading to decentralization and self-control of the individual. This system provides the research establishment with a profound sense of purpose and direction, which is essential for effective planning and control. The results-oriented MBO principles adopt the performance standards, in association with costs and manpower, value assessment, feedback, and improvement. Moreover, the wisely implemented MBO, with the necessary respect for creative work, it can enhance the job satisfaction of the research worker as well as the overall productivity of the research establishment.

Brumback and McFee (1982): MBO development and implementation in the U.S. Department of Health and Human Services. The author of this study asserts the uniqueness of their work to describe, develop and implement their MBO approach in the U.S. Department of Health and Human Services. Their three-years study integrates a two-fold performance appraisal into a broader performance management process. The proposed performance accounts for the individuals' behaviour on the job and the results achieved. The authors denote that performance planning to be the function most crucial for successful performance.

Ford and McLaughlin (1982): MBO structural analysis; MBO programs. This study is especially focuses on avoiding disappointment in MBO programs.

Hatfield (1982): MBO in the hospital management. In the present study MBO, and its concurring objections, are co-evaluated.

Johnson and McMurry (1982): MBO in the hospital management. MBO is particularly studied in the view of its introducer Drucker's management by objective concept.

Kenneth and Lampi (1982): MBO in the healthcare sector. The study presents the MBO function in the business office, regarding the particular traits of the healthcare sector.

Martin et al. (1982): MBO in the healthcare sector. The MBO attempts to introduce the management to the new-born (at the time of the study's publication) management application to the medical personnel. The specific MBO application is in the field of a surgical residency team.

Murphy and Redden (1982): MBO in in medical education enrichment programs. The scope of this study is overcome the difficult in evaluating the effectiveness of numerous medical education enrichment programs that have been established throughout the United States. Despite the programs goals' existence, yet most program managers do not have a simple tool for transforming these broad statements into measurable performance standards, unless a goal clarification process is initiated. Therefore, the study regards MBO as an appropriate process for refining a program's goals that enables the fair evaluation of these enrichment programs.

Weihrich (1982): MBO and strategic career

management. The publication period of this present study coincides to a critical standpoint of MBO theory. Therefore, the present study attempts to reveal the critical traits of MBO by introducing the strategic career management to successfully MBO implementation.

Weihrich and Thomsen (1982): MBO structural analysis; MBO and Data-based research collaboration. This study utilizes the existing MBO characteristics by applying a data-based research. The ultimate scope is the improvement of the former (MBO's) traits.

Gruner (1983): MBO and employment.This study correlates the phenomenon of employment discrimination in MBO systems. This phenomenon is also reported in the view of the labour law legislation.

Kelly (1983): MBO structural analysis; Remedial MBO. This study examines the remedial prosperity of sustainable MBO theory.

Kordick (1983): MBO and quality assurance system. This study provides a quality assurance system based on MBO.

Mills (1983): MBO cooperation with task-centered system for mental healthcare facilities. Mental health facilities have apparently influenced from a variety of groups for recognition in the decision-making processes. The study positions earlier conceptions of MBO as either ill suited for social service agencies or not allowing for or encouraging involvement of the service consumer in the process. The study introduces the Social Service Model of Management by Objectives as an approach which can be used as a planning and communication tool for staff, administration, and the board with on-going input from clients and potential clients. The study concludes that, firstly utilizing client input through the problem identification process of the task-centred system in order to enhance the measurability of objectives in mental health facilities. This approach can also further staff identification with and involvement in agency functioning.

Moore and Scott (1983): MBO in a public agency In this study, Black and White managers, supervisors, and professionals of the City of Detroit transportation system consists the sampling population. The participants they had been involved with an annual MBO project. Explanations derived from the racial demographics of the organization, the MBO installation, and characteristics of MBO as a management process in public agencies are also presented.

Noble (1983): MBO In Hospital Pharmacy Management. This study evaluated the key – topics involved in hospital pharmacy management.

Pollok (1983): MBO in nursing In this study, MBO traits are adaptable to the nursing service setting. Managers responsible for nursing service units exploit MBO elements of formulation of goals and objectives, development of action plans, and implementation necessary to increase the accountability and the output of the work rendered. MBO for the nursing service is evaluated as a logical system of results and proven value.

Swiss (1983): MBO structural analysis; The interactions between the power shifts and personality under federal MBO. This study points out the detrimental effect of MBO shifted-power to the secretary office in part by documenting a "cycle of failure" for subordinates and by lessening the influence of outside groups. The study argues the normative case of welcoming the above type of shift and the determining affection of secretarial personality – which is expressed by him or her to value their internal power – for MBO success. As the study notably denotes:"Information is power in a large organization, and MBO forces information (particularly bad news) up to the secretarial level".

Fain and Sheathelm (1984): MBO administrative tool in nursing service . administrators This study points out the role of nursing leadership to minimize frustration among staff and optimize nursing effectiveness and job satisfaction. A manager administrator is called upon time and time again to increase the productivity to staff, by handling potent conflict between the organization's goals and the individual staff member's needs. MBO is not considered a mechanical or dehumanizing approach, but one that recognizes the importance of human relations to effective administration. MBO motives are the notions of "democratic procedures", "involvement", and "motivational techniques" and MBO prerequisites are a considerable amount of time and energy, in addition to organizational support. The study concludes considering MBO as an approach within a system, it provides a major organizational advantage-improved planning.

Fisher (1985): MBO concepts embodied in Optimized Production Technology (OPT). This study examines the underlying assumptions of both MBO and the traditional goal-setting techniques typically applied during the optimized implementation of just-in-time and Zero Inventory Systems. Moreover, a set of application rules and tools for both goal-setting and performance evaluation is introduced.

Williams (1985): MBO and Zero-Base Budgeting (ZBB) systems complementarity. This study argues the existence of popular arguments in the management literature advocating the implementation congruity and complementarity of both ZBB and MBO systems. Moreover, the management perceptions on ZBB implementation variables for MBO users and non-MBO users gathered from managers at two hierarchical levels within a single private sector organization are examined. Both univariate and multivariate tests indicate that ZBB implementation was not facilitated by the existence of an MBO system for either lower level management or for upper level management. The evidence obtained here strongly suggests that ZBB design implementation issues need to be thoroughly re-assessed, with the emphasis on matching compatible systemic properties between information sub-systems.

Deegan 2nd and O'Donovan (1986): MBO use to the healthcare of hypertension administration. MBO approach is funding and used to improve the detection and quality of treatment of hypertensive patients. This MBO approach, when accompanied by regular feedback, appears to motivate primary case teams, in order to improve the detection of hypertension in their patients.

Bozis (1986): MBO and medical group practice. MBO is both theoretically and practically determined via three primary functions of objective setting, objective using, and employee involvement. MBO in medical group practice could be proved beneficial when properly introduced. MBO approach falls beyond an academic concept, revealing its major strength in its recognition of the importance of human resources in implementing its function.

Kost (1986): MBO instalment in an academic medical center containing clinical laboratory divisions. MBO was installed in the author's institution in clinical laboratory divisions meeting prerequisites and fit the system to the local management environment. MBO is proved beneficial to improving communication, organizational clarity, planning for deadlines, motivation of participants, work load distribution, and productivity. Moreover, projects are easier to visualize, track, and coordinate. MBO optimum functions with one- to two-year-long projects, involving problem solving and innovation. Finally, MBO is recommended for other academic medical center laboratories, provided executive management commits the necessary time and resources to install MBO carefully as a relatively loose, locally administered form of management philosophy, rather than management technology.

Seyna (1986): MBO structural analysis; MBO: its comprehensive definition gains diversified benefits. This study positions a continuing controversy about the meaning of MBO and whether it has been of value, in the reference publication year. The author argues that most of the problems have been due to the lack of a generally accepted definition. A new and comprehensive definition, based on MBO "introducer" Peter Drucker's original work on the subject, is presented. The proposed definition will help organizations use MBO to increase productivity, improve quality, lower costs, make faster decisions and serve customers better.

Friesen (1987): MBO structural analysis; MBO, managerial effectiveness, and efficiency interactions. The components and dimensions of an individual or organization as an operating entity are described and suggestions for better management are proposed. Managerial effectiveness and efficiency are also defined.

Lively (1987): MBO application in hospital pharmacy management. This study shows the main MBO topics regarding the hospital pharmacy management.

Maguire (1987): MBO and nursing. This study investigates the MBO application of its principles in the nursing sector.

Adorian et al. Jeffers (1988): MBO in the healthcare sector. This study reveals the potent MBO use in the radiation oncology center.

Williams and Hinings (1988): MBO structural analysis; MBO revisiting in combination to matching control system implications and organizational characteristics. The implementation of new control systems governed by a rational-technical logic is influenced from the underlying value and belief structures lodged within prevailing control systems, task and hierarchy. The present study denotes several prescriptive implications offering for the design of systems change, such as the discordance facing the context of MBO and zero-base budgeting (ZBB) complementarity.

Racz and Simon (1990): MBO in the healthcare sector. This study relates the MBO application in the Szabadsaghegy children's sanatorium of Budapest.

Benson and Townes (1990): QMBO application to the healthcare sector. This study is positioned critically to existing MBO standard tool in the managerial inventory, since the Department of Ambulatory Care Services in Methodist Hospital of Indiana (USA) is proved detrimental to each daily operation. Alternatively, the study proposes the suitability of the Quality Management By Objectives "QMBO" as a viable tool to the examined healthcare system sustainability.

Braithwaite et al. (1991): MBO and healthcare institutions. An evaluation of MBO approach with particular reference to health care institutions is presented and the disadvantages this approach are discussed. A more comprehensive performance management system than MBO is advocated. The study outcomes reveal that experience provides guidelines by which senior managers may successfully implement goal-directed performance management programs in health care institutions, in order to enhance organisational effectiveness and the goal-oriented behaviour of managers.

Buj Fernández et al. (1991): MBO in hospital management. The study investigates the MBO application of its principles in training all-round nurses in Spain district.

Rodgers and Hunter (1991): MBO structural analysis; Organizational productivity outcomes in combination of MBO. The successful combination of the processes of goal setting, participation in decision making, and objective feedback with MBO, have each been shown to increase productivity. One factor that is predicted to be essential to success is the level of top-management commitment to MBO. Additionally, results of the meta-analysis show that when top-management commitment was high the average gain in productivity is more than 9 times higher comparing to the average productivity when commitment is low.

Pearson and Reyes (1991): Effective clinical education methodology by using MBO. Educational programs must ensure that students continue to receive appropriate clinical education. The present study applies the MBO simple technique that has been successful in ensuring appropriate clinical education at the institution of the authors is discussed.

Paez (1993): MBO features of quality policy, drug prescription, drug distribution, drug administration. This study examines: A) the implementation of an Improvement Plan for the quality of the drug prescription, dispensing and administration process at a regional hospital. The MBO is planning to: a) Improve the quality of how medical prescription is filled out. B) Eradicate errors due to the way medical orders are transcribed by nursing staff. C) Eradicate errors due to the way drugs are dispensed by the Pharmacy Service. D) Record drug prescription and administration in the Emergency Department on a specific form. E) Evaluate the importance of returns of uncalled for drugs (not administered), making corrective decisions on the spot. Analysis of the results supports the future

Gunn (1995): MBO contribution for healthcare administrators. The study handles the necessity of hospital and clinics in terms of delivering effective, efficient healthcare that it is undergoing rapid change. The study demonstrates how strategic planning can contribute to that end.

Tan et al. (1997): MBO and nursing. This study investigates the MBO application of its principles in training all-round nurses in China district.

Busch (1998): MBO structural analysis; Relationship among the concepts of MBO, self-efficacy and goal commitment. This study investigates the relationship among the concepts of self-efficacy, the goal commitment, and the knowledge about the MBO programme. The results revealed that self-efficacy in improving productivity and commitment to productivity goals are both positively correlated to attitudes towards MBO. There is no significant correlation between participation and attitudes towards MBO. The study establishes self-efficacy and goal commitment as significant constructs in explaining attitudes towards MBO in the public administration.

Ricci et al. (1999): MBO application in national healthcare service. This study presents the introduction of MBO in the management of National Health Service, being especially experienced from the USL 2 Pentria Agency.

Tatarkin (2001): MBO in conjunction to market management mechanisms. The study investigates the collaboration of both MBO and market management mechanisms for regional (particularly Ural) development.

Zahraee (2003): MBO approach to evaluating university faculty. MBO approach, reflecting the Human Resource practice of performance plans and evaluations in corporate America, is used for the design, analysis and implementation of a faculty evaluation system in both departments of Electrical Engineering Technology and Manufacturing Engineering Technologies and Supervision at Purdue University Calumet. This new system asks faculty to set goals and objectives with some degree of flexibility and is in line with the accreditation requirement changes of Accreditation Board for Engineering and Technology (ABET).

Dahlsten et al. (2005): Car manufacturing companies using internally-oriented MBO. This study aims at studying a car company volume target, regarding the consequences it has on organisational practices. Interviews with relevant managers at the company were conducted. Interpretations of a seemingly clear objective showed different views on both the rationale for and possible direction of the needed change. Moreover, an increasing gap between middle and top managers are organisational responses to the demanding volume ambition. The study deals with long-term objectives, suggesting that the lack of academic research interest in the MBO discourse is misleading and that management researchers should examine how existing of renewal of research on MBO is used in practice. Organisations rely on objectives, but such objectives need to be translated into detailed actions by top management. The creation of meaning and actual means to fulfil the targets is an important dimension to consider for managers wanting to manage the organisation by using objectives. Organisational context and cultural obstacles must not be neglected.

Antoni (2005): The role of MBO to team working effectiveness. MBO is considered as a means for leading self-regulating teams. The function and effectiveness of MBO systems are investigated. Particularly, the MBO system of a company in the construction supply industry is analysed. The exploration of the mechanisms and the effects of MBO at team level are materialized by testing a model for group goal setting. Group goal commitment and group goals moderated by task interdependence are supposed to influence group processes as a mediating variable for group effectiveness. Results do not consistently support this model. The moderating effect of task interdependence could not be supported. The consequences for developing a model for MBO at team level and implementing effective MBO systems are discussed.

Cai and Hu (2005): MBO application in drug administration of hospital pharmacy. This study implements MBO in the process of drug administration, in order to raise the managing level of the hospital pharmacy and improve professional quality of staff. Objective systems were built in outpatientdepartment, inpatient-department and emergency pharmacies. The correspondence between the accounts and the numbers of the drugs, and the error rates of checking cost were the examination indexes. The study revealed that MBO deserves to be widely used in drug administration of hospital pharmacy

Wibeck et al. (2006): Integration of ecological concerns into national, political and administrative structures, in conjunction to MBO technique. MBO technique could be appropriate for integrating ecological concerns into national political and administrative structures. The study examines communicative aspects of environmental MBO, looking specifically at the implementation, administration, and assessment of Swedish environmental quality objectives. The proposed methodology is illustrated by quotations from individual and focus group interviews, and the possibility of communicative arising problems is also commented. In assessing the achievement of environmental objectives, indicators are used as communicative tools. The investigation of whether and how these indicators contribute to the de- and recontextualization of environmental objectives is also discussed.

Sohn et al. (2007): Information system and MBO collaboration to R&D projects implementation. This study investigates the way of MBO to achieve successful implementation of massive research and development projects requiring collaboration among industries, universities and government-supported research institute. An engineering process innovation model, based on information system, implements a real-world web-based project (objective) management system. Overall effect is analyzed through the webbased-approaching questionnaires. The scope of the above approach is to observe how well the system and its generated information meet requirements on the ultimate impact of the system upon objective management and communication. The questionnaire on the system effect reveals that the information system is useful to objective management and communication, and that the quality of the system is more than acceptable as well. The responses to the questionnaires are subject to improving those in-depth interviews.

Concepción (2008): MBO structural analysis; MBO in the light of creativity and conceptual clarity. In this study the need of co-application of MBO with creativity and conceptual clarity is investigated.

Elvik (2008): MBO approach for road safety national planning. The Norwegian Public Roads Administration has developed a comprehensive system of road safety MBO. A broad set of objectives regarding road user behaviour, vehicle safety standards and the safety of roads has been formulated as part of the National Transport Plan for the term 2010-2019. The study describes the system of reducing fatalities and serious injuries and provides a critical analysis of it. Factors that influence the effectiveness of management by objectives are identified. It is concluded that while the system of management by objectives developed in Norway has a number of attractive characteristics it also has a number of weak points that may limit its effectiveness.

Cao et al. (2009): Power supply reliability based on a distribution network GIS platform. Specific codes introduction describes completely the topological structure of distribution network which is necessary for MBO. Additionally, a new algorithm used in objective decomposition for power supply reliability is designed. The factors which can influence the results of objective decomposition are discussed and determined. The algorithm is integrated in power distribution network

GIS platform, showing that the decomposition algorithm can obviously improve the reliability of power supply.

Jia et al. (2009): Human error rate assessment for power companies. Human error is the key reason of accidents in power companies. Approaching the problem of how to impartially evaluate the human error rate of power companies and the branches, the concept of contribution rate is given, in order to embody the effect of branches under the particular condition including the surrounding and their task according to the MBO theory. A mathematical programming model is founded to get the due human error rate of power companies and to evaluate the branches' contribution to the company.

Li et al. (2009): Quality Management By Objectives (QMBO) for product manufacturing process. The evaluation problem to rationally assign Quality Management By Objectives (QMBO) throughout the execution process of relevant product manufacturing departments is approached with a three-step methodology of the establishment, decomposition and evaluation of quality objectives. Firstly, the product quality objectives are established and selected by using the method of Quality Function Deployment (QFD). The results of an aircraft manufacturing enterprise application prove that it is effective to guarantee the realization of enterprise quality objectives.

Pavlova and Afanasieva (2009): Decision tree and MBO effective methods from the point of view of healthcare economics. In Bulgaria, general practitioners who give primary medical care have to accomplish their mission in condition of insufficient financial resources. The approaches of "decision tree" and "management by objectives" are implemented through filling in a questionnaire. Equal opportunities concerning medical qualification, conditions of work the knowledge of modern economic approaches are also considered advantageous to general practitioners medical treatment.

Roth (2009): MBO structural analysis, critic upon MBO obsolescence. The corporate dogma of MBO for many decades is criticised in the view of its touted strengths rapidly becoming liabilities in the new global century, as more empowering and flexible approaches sprout up as promising new models for performance management. The study examines the dampening effect MBO can have on creativity, teamwork, and the ability to respond to changes in the business. Moreover two cases of organizations that broke out of the mould are also presented.

Lee and Ahn (2010): Hospital Nursing. This study is designed to develop performance evaluation key indicators (PEKIs) for management by objectives (MBO) and to estimate their weights for hospital nurses. PEKIs and their main weights – placing in the order of: customer satisfaction, patient education, direct nursing care, profit increase, and safety management – can be utilized for impartial evaluation and MBO for hospital nurses. Further research to verify PEKIs would lead to successful implementation of MBO.

Concluding Remarks: Among 82 literature survey, it is found that that the main area of MBO application is in the medical sector. The four main medical sub-groupings that is, healthcare, nursing, hospital management and hospital pharmacy account for 40% of the total references. The gathered studies were also presented and succinctly analyzed, in order to reveal the favourable and unfavourable areas of application by using the MBO approach.

7.4   CONCLUDING REMARKS

We have discussed that MBO was first expounded by Peter Drucker; in the 1950s with reference to business management and since then his writings have influenced management practice on both sides of the Atlantic and the technique has been introduced into scores of companies, British and American over past five decades. It is important to note that its influence however, has not been confined to the manufacturing spheres but has been adopted by many sectors of the economy and essential services, for instance,   Local Education Authorities, Higher Education institutions, Health Authorities, and   branches of the Civil Service at various times. Basically, said Drucker, in the practice of management, "objectives are needed in every area where performance and results directly and vitally affect the service and prosperity of the business."

Originally   the   concept   was   intended   for application   at   three   levels   in   an   organization: to corporate objectives, to departments, and to individual objectives, but later these ideas were developed further in Britain by J,W. Humble in his books, Improving Management   Performance   and   Management   By Objectives while   retaining   the   same   elements   as Drucker. For Humble, MBO is "a dynamic system which seeks to integrate the company`s need to clarify and achieve its profit and growth goals with the manager's need to contribute and develop her/himself.

It   is   a   demanding   and   rewarding   style   of managing a business". Since the middle sixties what has been   added   is   rather   experience   in   modus   operandi than   conceptual   development   except   perhaps   in   the sphere of education. Finally the complete MBO system is to get managers and empowered employees acting to implement and achieve their plans, which automatically achieve those of the organisation.

Chapter 8

OTHER MANAGEMENT SYSTEMS CLOSELY RELATED TO MBO

8.1   MANAGEMENT BY PARTICIPATION (MBP)

Management participation leads to peaceful evaluation of economic system on a democratic basis in which managers and workers (or subordinates) participate in the task of finding the best solutions to the problems faced by the business.   This type of management methods has many inherent benefits, particularly in the areas of higher productivity and sound industrial relations. The necessity to give the workers and managers the places as partners in the industry is more and more recognized. By using this approach the workers and managers are closely associated with the top management and feel operation of the enterprise their own concern. They provide positive contribution to accomplishment of the objectives of their organization. This approach helps a great deal in meeting the psychological needs of the workers, gives them an actual knowledge about economic and technical position, and brings them closer to the management.

There are various methods and techniques of workers' participation in management which can be used. Some of the salient ones are as follows:

Joint Committees: Joint committees are formed consisting of representatives of workers and management with an express aim to weld the work force and the management in a single mould. Such committees discuss and advise on various organization matters of the enterprises (excluding matters concerning collective bargaining). The types of committees may include Budget Committee, Cost/Profit Optimization Committee, Job Evaluation Committee, Recruitment Committee, etc. This method open the way for higher morale & workers motivation, leading to greater productivity and cordial human relations.

Suggestion Scheme: By this scheme, workers are given opportunities to put their ideas forward, which may have conceived or perceived during the performance of their operations. Such scheme should also include reward inducement to encourage workers to take more interest in the scheme. Experience has shown that sometimes the suggestions received have been of immense value for the business.

Co-Partnership: There are co-operatives which have successfully operated for years, In such scheme workers are issued shares of the enterprise and are made as shareholders thus enabling them to elect their representatives to the Board of Directors to participate in the management of the organization.

There are various distinct advantages of management by participation, some important ones include as follows:

(a)   A useful channel of communication is created which helps in maintaining harmonious relations between workers and management.

(b)   Useful and productive ideas can be pooled and implemented for the benefit of the enterprise.

(c)   Co-ordinate between the activities of a number of related functions is improved.

(d)   Problems can be solved by discussion by the committees, thus inter-personal conflicts are minimised.

(e)   Full advantages of specialisation can be utilised.

(f)   The responsibility is shared instead of being borne by one person, thus stress is minimised.

However, this approach too is not free from disadvantages as committees are more time consuming and also lack of sincerity in decision making may emerge due to divided responsibilities.

8.2   MANAGEMENT BY FEEDBACK (MBF)

The author has perceived this system which is based on the assumption that generally people are shy and nervous about expressing their opinion, suggestion or problem openly due to fear of intimidation. However, if the same type of people are given the opportunity to express themselves through a secret ballot box without any chance of being identified, the ideas, suggestions and opinion will start to flow. This proposed system in practice should be installed as follows:

An organizational Audit Committee should be formed, consisting of members drawn from the staff functional group (as against line managers) reporting directly to the top management. This committee should review the feedback data received through two secret ballot boxes out of which one ballot box installed for complaints and problems, whilst the other for opinions and suggestions for improvement). If feedback information is of serious nature, the audit committee should initiate verification procedure through questionnaire or personal interviews or other suitable method. The audit committee should then prepare a report for top management with recommendations for corrective/development actions. The process should be repeated periodically, preferably after three months period. In the light of the recommendations made by the audit committee, the top management should adjust their policies accordingly for the benefit of the organization and the worker alike. However, this system may contribute to organizational conflicts, but these may be eliminated or at least minimized by communicating the objectives at all levels of the organization.

8.3 MANAGEMENT BY WALKING AROUND (MBWA)

It is surprising to know that how much one can learn from the informal exchanges (or personal observation) through the management by walking around technique (MBWA) which calls for the manager to get out of his (or her) office and be in touch with the operational team.

Tom Peters and his co-authors in both publications namely: 'A Passion of Excellence' and 'In search of Excellence' make special emphasis on the importance of MBWA.[39] For example in 'A Passion for Excellence', Peters and Austin refer MBWA as 'being in touch' in the following words; MBWA means, us being in touch, with customers, suppliers, and people. It facilitates innovation, and makes possible the teaching of values to every member of an organization. Listening, facilitating,

---

[39] Peters, Tom, and Nancy Austin.- 'A Passion for Excellence: The Leadership Difference'/ New York: Random House, 1985.

and teaching and reinforcing values. What is this except leadership?[40]

Koonlz, O'Donnel, and Weihrick stress that managers should not only rely solely on the management information system to assess or measure the progress of their work units but also through personal observation, They state in these words: "In any preoccupation with the devices of managerial control, one should never overlook the importance of control through personal observation. Budgets, charts, reports, ratios, auditor's recommendations, and other devices are essential to control. But the manager who relies wholly on these devices and sits, so to speak, in a soundproof control room reading dials and manipulating levers can hardly expect to do a thorough job of control".[41]

Some managers believe that MBWA is not desirable as people may think that management is snooping on them and may cause resentment. However, if MBWA is having suggestive and positive approach of the manager with a view to engage in a genuine dialogue with his subordinates will receive welcoming response. However, MBWA has some constraints such as the following:

> ➢ MBWA must not disrupt the organizational chain of command. The researchers have found that for the effective functioning of any organization, a reasonable chain of command must exist for maintaining a reasonable balance between

---

[40] Peters, Tom, and Nancy Austin.- 'A Passion for Excellence: The Leadership Difference'/ New York: Random House, 1985, p. 31.

[41] Koontz, Harold, Cyril OíDonnell, and Heinz Weirich.- 'Management'/ New York: McGraw-Hill Book Company, 1980, pp. 759-760

freedom and structure of the organization. If chain of command is too loose, a state of confusion and uncertainty results. On the other hand, if chain of command is too rigid, a state of loss in initiative and creativity results. Therefore, managers should follow the common sense approach with mindfulness that MBWA should not disrupt the normal chain of command.

➢ Managers must take MIS & MBWA as two essential instruments in gauging the Progress of their subordinates and ensure that MIS is an accurate reflection of MBWA.

MBWA has a most appropriate application in Project Management environment where 'being in touch' with the Project team is one of the essential requisites of the Project Manager's task.

8.4 THEORY Z

Among contemporary management perspectives, Theory 'Z', as expounded by William Ouchi is his classic book 'Theory Z, 1981) is an attempt to integrate common business practices in type 'A, (American) organizations and Type 'J' Japanese) organizations. In Theory 'Z' approach, the key to increased productivity is to get employees involved by using various techniques, such as: interpersonal skills, quality circles, employees' development, etc. Ouchi felt that Japanese industrial success was a result of better management which places more emphasis on long-range planning, strong employer-employees loyalty, and consensus decision making, etc. and concluded that some Japan organizations could serve as a model for American organization. However, Ouchi and others have pointed out that not all Japanese techniques can be used in American settings. But nevertheless, it is expected that Theory 'Z' management will become increasingly popular in the coming years.

Under the framework of Theory 'Z', William D. Hitt has suggested a six stepped process by advocating that theory 'Z' approach to MBO can correct the deficiencies embedded in the traditional approach· These steps are: preparation for MBO Process (Step 1); Develop of Organizational Objectives (step 2); Development of Department/Section/Group Objectives (step 3); Development of Performance Objectives (step 4); Interim Review of all Objectives (step 5); and Cumulative Review of all Objectives (step 6)[42]

Hitt believes that inherent value of this six step MBO process is that it produces both coherent and commitment, which is what theory "Z" is all about.

8.5 MANAGEMENT BY EXCEPTION (MBE)

The Management by exception comprises of a systematic approach of handling the management problems through a system of Identification and Communication that signals the manager as to when and where attention is needed. This approach frees the manager from the demands of routine activities and enables the manager to devote more time to creative efforts directed towards improving the overall efficiency and effectiveness of the organization. The main object of this system is to focus attention of the manager on analyzing the situation, identifying & isolating the critical problems demanding decision and action, and taking timely and qualitative decisions based on the rapidly available information. Under this system, the manager receives only condensed, and invariable comparative reports covering all segments of the business including

---

[42]Hitt, William D.- 'Management in Action: Guidelines for New Managers'/ Columbus, Ohio: Battlelle Press, 1984, pp. 107-109

all the exceptions to the past averages. This readily available information gives him a global view in a matter of only few minutes. The manager then makes a careful analysis of existing records and standards of performance in a systematic way, by utilizing the experience or the knowledge of the past attainments. Evaluation of this system may be considered as Six Phase Process as shown in Fig. 6.6. The phases include: (i) Measure Phase; (ii) Projection Phase; (iii) Selection Phase;(iv) Observation Phase; (v) Comparison Phase; and (vi) Action Phase.

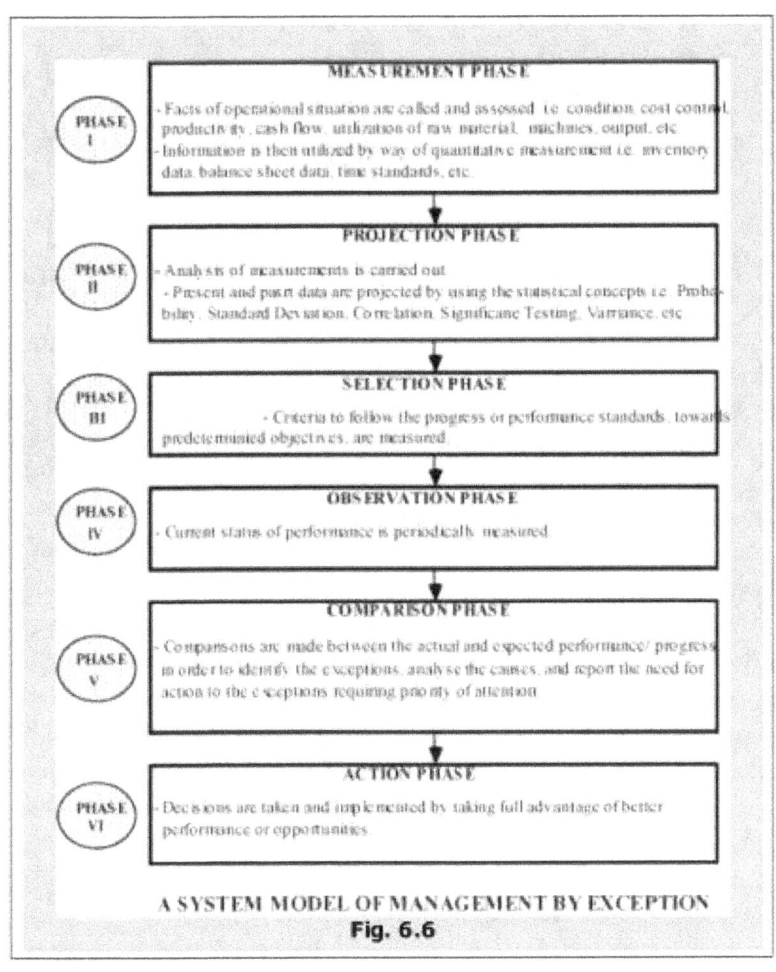

A SYSTEM MODEL OF MANAGEMENT BY EXCEPTION

Fig. 6.6

Management By Objectives (MBO) in Enterprises

The Manager By Exception (MBE) system has many inherent benefits, the more salient ones are as follows:

> ➢ It save considerable time of the managers who stands to deal problems at a particular point of time and concentrate on efforts of solving critical problems and making timely decisions.
> ➢ It calls for lesser number of decisions which enables the manager to go into more detail for critical issues.
> ➢ It enables a manager to increase his span of control and related activities.
> ➢ It enables the management to fully utilize, historic records, past trends and available data for projecting the improved Performance/Progress.
> ➢ It alerts the management on critical issues and points out both the specially good and the specially bad exceptions (i.e. good opportunities as well as difficulties).
> ➢ It prevents the management from over managing and thereby causes less stress on the managers.
> ➢ It provides both qualitative and quantitative standards for judging the current position of the business.

However, this method too is not free from disadvantages and limitations. Some of these include: (i) it increases paper work, and requires a comprehensive observing and reporting system; (ii) it is silent till the problem becomes critical, and (iii) it provide no guidelines to measure some important factors, like human behaviour.

Chapter 9

MBO AND STRATEGIC MANAGEMENT

9.1   INTRODUCTION

As we have discussed above, since the nineteen fifties management by objectives (MBO) has been a vehicle for motivation, evaluation and control for many businesses both small and large. MBO features a systematic approach to change that stresses the achievement of results by directing individual efforts toward attainable objectives.

These efforts involved agreed upon objectives between the manager and the subordinate. Once objectives are agreed upon, the subordinate implements the activities to achieve the desired results, while the manager periodically evaluates, and hopefully, clarifies the path for the subordinates in meetings.

These meetings emphasized two person relationships, which enhance individual growth on one hand, but may have provided counterproductive results given the culture of the organization and the recent development of strategic management systems.

In the current business environment, many corporations have embraced a form of MBO and at the same time these same corporations have more recently adopted strategic management, as a process of motivation and control.

9.2 MANAGEMENT BY OBJECTIVES (MBO) AS A MANAGEMENT TOOL

MBO system in its idealistic form is a management tool which can help managers to accomplish the prescription as outlined above by combining of objective setting, planning, control, and reward systems, all of which are so crucial to effective strategy formulation and its implementation.

Management By Objectives (MBO) is a style of management of an organization, which emphasises the achievement of results expressed in terms of objective. In MBO process both supervisor and subordinate jointly set overall organizational goals and define each individual's area of responsibility in terms of the expected results. These measures are then used as guidelines for operating the respective organizational unit and also performance appraisal of its members.

However, there is a strong constraint attached to the MBO process that objectives must be specific, time bound, realistic, quantitative, qualitative and measurable. In essence, MBO emphasis the importance of subordinates' setting specific objectives, with the help and concurrence of their supervisors that are intended to be achieved within the period mutually decided upon, and then having their performance measured against the pre-set objectives.

Research of Robert H. Mills in an engineering & research environment, has identified that a direct relationship existed between experiencing ambiguity and job tension, personal ineffectiveness, job dissatisfaction and unfavourable attitude towards work associates; and suggest that to reduce these industrial ailments, a program of MBO would be appropriate[43]. Because MBO is based on better communication, co-operation and participation by all levels in the organization, it can realise benefits to all organizational participants. This is why both managers and subordinates often welcome it alike.

MBO is behavioural approach to management in which emphasis is placed more on relationships, than positions and information flow is both ways (unlike conventional approach in which information flow is priority downward and emphasis is on positions rather than relationships). Therefore, MBO approach provides a better co-ordination among various organizational units and leads to better understanding between the superiors and the subordinates. There are six elements of 'MBO' Process which may be considered critical to the successful implementation of 'MBO'. The process is shown in Fig. 6.2 above.

The process starts with good preparation including orientation to all members of the management team with an emphasis that active involvement in the 'MBO' program is an integral part of each manager's job. The next step is to communicate organization goals (including the CEO directive) to subordinates at each level of organization hierarchy and review/discuss the superior's important job responsibilities, followed by the discussion and joint agreement on key effectiveness of components of subordinate's job. Once understanding is built up regarding responsibilities and obligations of both superior and subordinates, next step is to jointly set objective, targets and performance criteria followed by interim progress review and finally evaluating

[43] Mills, Robert H.- 'How Job Conflict and Ambiguity Affect R & D Professionals'/ Research Management, Vol. XVIII, No. 4, July 1975.

performance and distribution rewards with a feedback to the process for further developed.

Although MBO holds great promise as a powerful management tool, in impressing managerial effectiveness but nevertheless in actual practice it is vested with numerous pitfalls and shortcomings, resulting in a number of managers holding a negative view towards its implementations. Therefore, for each manager there is a challenge to build on the strength of MBO and or overcome its pitfalls. To achieve these twofold goals, managers should follow the guidelines suggested by Harold Koontz in his book: 'Shortcomings and Pitfalls in Managing by objectives'[44]. Emphasising a conscientious application of these guidelines, Harold Koontz advocates the importance of MBO as a comprehensive system of management in the following words.

"Management by objectives must be a way of managing, a way of planning as well as the key to organizing, staffing, directing, and controlling - it is then a part of managing, a summary of what has been done, and not a difficult separate operation"[45].

MBO, though it can be a very useful tool for effective management, but it is not a panacea for all organizational ailments as Martin and Shell quite rightly expressed in the following worlds.

"Management by objectives is not a panacea, but it can be a very useful tool in improving managerial

---

[44] Koontz, Harold.- 'Shortcomings and Pitfall in Managing by Objectives'/ Management By Objectives, Jan. 1972, pp.6-12.

[45] Koontz, Harold.- 'Making Managerial Appraisal Effective'/ California Management Review, Vol. 15, No. 2, Winter 1972, p. 51.

effectiveness in the engineering and scientific environment. While it is not easily applied, there is considerable evidence to suggest that technical organizations can benefit from a well-planned and functioning management by objectives program[46].

8.3 RECENT STRATEGIC THINKING IN ORGANIZATIONAL CONTEXT

The researches have found that the structures and studies that support strategic management as, by and large, the status of MBO systems exists within an organization that practices strategic planning. In parallel to the development and evolution of MBO (Fig. 6.5), strategic thinkg also emerged, the status of which during last two decades is discussed herein below:

1992 : The CEO as organization designer, 'in an interview with Prof. Jay W. Forrester' concluded that: " in a complex world, to "design" means to rethink the logic of cause and effect."

1993: In February, on the question on 'think local, organize ... question, new evidence suggested that the most popular routes to global success are not always reliable, whilst in August on 'balancing corporate power' a new federalist paper (winner of the McKinsey Award for the best article) published in the Harvard Business Review in 1992 provided answer to - how complex modern organizations can achieve unity without uniformity.

1994: In May on Fallacies in organizing for performance, a brief introduction to the most common

---

[46] Martin, Desmond D. and Richard L. Shell.- 'What Every Engineer should know about Human Resources Management'/ New York: Marcel Dekker, Inc. p. 156

assumptions that lead astray efforts to boost performance was provided.

1996: In February on the question: what is wrong with the consumer goods organization, a new category-based structure was born, whist in August two companies (Ford and Kraft) got it right 'flatness forays' on reorganizing around processes and finding the answetr to the question: how much functional structure should be left in place?

1998: In February on ' the new economics of organization' in their purest forms, the coordination of markets motivate and hierarchies, the technique to combine the best of both were achieved, thereby accepting the two challenges for the corporations of the future: entrepreneurialism and knowledge.

1999: In Noevember, through the dialog: 'can a company ever be too big', conflictiong views emerged as some people believed that "it is different this time." Others did not.

2001: In February on 'beyond the business unit', it was recognized that corporate organization's future lied in the ability to work across business units and concluded that opportunity-based organizational design may help to achieve success. In May on 'organization growth', as drivers of corporate success, organizational design and the quality of leadership shared pride of place with strategy, wholst 'the innovative organization'the trick was found to balance partitioning and integration in answer to the question: how new companies can grow quickly without sacrificing performance discipline. In August, on 'beyond the unbundled corporation'it was realized that a new business model may forever change the way companies compete; whilst on 'making solution the answer', many companies hard-pressed to maintain their margins through products alone are turning to 'solutions.' But to succeed, they must not only embrace competitors but also often turn away existing customers; and on managing the knowledge manager', it was discovered than before developing and executing agenda, it is imperative to agree on what you want to achieve. In the same month on 'the future of the network company', it was found that even during the slowdown, networked companies   outperforming   conventional   ones   with prospectus to go on doing so.

2002: In   June, on 'Just-in-time strategy for a turbulent world', uncertainty and rising levels of risk made it impossible for companies to determine the future and found out that a portfolio-of-initiatives approach to strategy can help ensure that companies take full advantage of their best opportunities without taking unnecessary risks. In December 2002 on ' who is accouuntavle for IT, it was found that who were business leaders.

2003: In June, on ' knowledge management comes to philanthropy', ir was found that Foundations were endowed with intellectual as well as financial capital, thereby then was   the time to use it. On 'organization helping people pull together', it was fond that even **in** the largest and best-managed companies, hundreds of organizational muddles took place every day, who throughout the economy, added up to a staggering   waste   of   national   resources.   On, 'organizational lessons for nonprofits', America learned the importance of building organizational capacity the hard way. On, 'the value in organization',it was established that CEOs must be more architect than general   and   took   the   tasks   to   design   working environments where thousands of people know what to do, cooperate to get it done, and experience it as personally fulfilling. On, 'when reorganization works, it was realized that even a corporate revamping inspired by state-of-the-art design principles won't succeed if not driven by a powerful, well-timed business idea adapted to social realities. In August on 'managing for improved corporate performance', generating great performance required a more dynamic approach to building and adapting a company's capabilities than merely squeezing its operations. On. 'what CEOs really think about IT',it was found that executives in France were taking a more proactive approach to ensure their IT investments bear fruit.

2004: in March on 'when efficient capital and operations go hand in hand', Olli-Pekka Kallasvuo, Nokia's head of mobile phones and a former CFO, discussed strategic organization, performance measurement, and the value of financial transparency. In July on, 'next-generations CIOs', to ensure that IT investments have the greatest impact, CIOs must involve business-unit leaders and concentrate on the big picture. In August on 'making a market in knowledge', it was determined that for companies and their employees alike, knowledge is power—and profit; whilst on' 'on organizing Customer Relationship Management (CRM)',it was determined that companies should treat a CRM solution as a product or service and its users as internal customers, by making it valuable, pricing appropriately, advertising, and providing after-sales support.In Novemeber on, 'organizing for effectiveness in public sector', it was found that traditional public-sector organizations can be redesigned to perform more successfully—even when market forces are lacking.

2005: In February on 'leadership as the starting point of strategy', it was found that even the best strategy can fail if a corporation doesn't have a cadre of leaders with the right capabilities at the right levels of the organization. In April on 'how to escape the short-term trap',it was determined that markets may expect solid performance over the short term, but they also value sustained performance over the long term, therby companies managing both time frames. In May on, 'global champions from emerging markets, it was found that developing economies had become an invaluable springboard for companies looking to compete successfully in foreign market. In July on, 'it was found that according to the McKinsey Global Survey of Business Executives, confidence was down, whilst distractions were up. In August on, 'building the healthy corporation',it was found that it wass difficult—but vital—for managers to strike a balance between the short and long terms strategies. In the same month on 'getting bigger' it was found that the world's largest companies were more successful than ever, but scale bringing its own challenges.

In the same month on, 'the 21st-century organizatios', it was found that big corporations must make sweeping organizational changes to get the best from their professionals. In the same month on, 'what its leaders do' it was found that companies that relied on IT governance systems alone will come up short. In November on 'improving productivity', it wad found that economic activity in developed economies was again undergwent a broad and deep shift; whilst on, 'strategy in an era of global giants', it was found that the world's biggest companies were learning to manage complexity; and on, 'the next revolution in interaction', it was found that successful efforts to exploit the growing importance of complex interactions could well generate durable competitive advantages.

2006: In Januuary on, 'ten trends to watch', it was found that macroeconomic factors, environmental and social issues, and business and industry developments will all profoundly shape the corporate landscape in the coming years. In February on, 'distortions and deceptions in strategic decisions', it was found that companies were vulnerable to misconceptions, biases, and plain old lies, but not hopelessly vulnerable; and on, 'the 'moment of truth' in customer service', it was found that focus on the interactions that are important to customers—and on the way frontline employees handled those interactions and executives should recognize and compensate for cognitive biases and agency problem; and on, 'the right service strategies for product companies', it was found that as products evolved into commodities, services became more important, but however, companies that play this new game must understand its rules; whist on, it was found that 'when organization isn't enough restructuring doesn't always lead to improved performance. In April on 'an executive take on the top budiness trendsL a McKinsey Global Survet', it was found that executives reported an accelerating pace of change in an increasingly competitive business environment, driven by knowledge and information trends and the forces of globalization.

In May on, 'competitive advantage from better interaction', it was found that tacit interactions are becoming central to economic activity, thereby making those who undertake them more effective isn't like tweaking a production line; whilst on. 'making a market in talent', it was found that a 21st-century company should put as much effort into developing its talented employees as it puts into recruiting them; and on, 'the adaptable corporation', it was found that to survive, organizations must execute in the present and adapt to the future and it was also found that only few of organizations manage to do both well.

In July on, 'building a nimble organization: a McKinsey Global Survey', it was found that executives saw an urgent need to increase the agility and speed of their organization and were trying in various ways to do so. In Agust on managing your organizations by the evidence', it was found that an organization was much more likely to improve its current performance and underlying health by using a combination of complementary practices rather than any one of them alone, according to new McKinsey research. In August, 'on mapping the value of employee collaboration', as collaboration within and among organizations became increasingly important, and recommended that companies must improve their management of the networks where it typically occurs.

In September on improving strategic planning: a McKinsey Survey', it was found that executives pointed out that their companies could be a lot more effective at developing a strategy and implementing strategic plans, whilst suggesting some areas for improvement. In November on, 'managing for growth: an interview with former Emerson CEO Chuck Knight', it was determined that the company's CEO from 1973 to 2000 explained how it transformed itself from a local manufacturer of simple components into a global technology giant.

2007: In January on what public companies can learn from private equity', it was found that Public companies will need to raise their governance game if they are to compete with private firms. In April on, ' acting on global trends: A McKinsey Global Survey', it was found that executives saw opportunities as well as risks in the global business landscape, yet many were not addressing them; whilst on, 'the role of networks in organizational change', it was found that companies shouldn't focus so much on formal structures while ignoring the informal ones. In May on, 'anatomy of a healthy corporation', it was found necessary to know the answer to the question: how can business leaders embed "healthy" thinking in the organization? Also on, 'better strategy through organizational design', it was found that redesigning an organization to take advantage of today's sources of wealth creation wasn't easy, but there can be no better use of a CEO's time; whilst on, 'building the civilized workplace', it was found that nasty people did not just make others feel miserable but also they created economic problems for their companies; and on, 'cracking the complexity code', it was found that there were two types of complexity and to manage them to creat value, understanding where to intervene is the key; whilst on, 'managing in a complex world', it was found that creating value from the challenges complexity presents was a major challenge confronting today's companies.

In July on, 'better strategy for business unit: a McKinsey Survey', it was found that executives were most positive about the outcomes of strategy formulation for their companies' business units when they work at companies that use a collaborative approach, and while they say following best practices yields better results, they use those practices less often than they think they should.

In August on, 'connecting employees to create value in investment banks' it was found that leaders used to have few options for changing their companies, except focusing on financial performance and walking the halls, which was no longer true; whilst on, 'the link between profit and organizational performance', McKinsey research indicated that organizational and financial performance were strongly mutually related.

In September on spurring value creation in IT services: an interviewing with the chairman of Indea's

Satyan Computers', the founder and chairman of Satyam detailed the philosophy that has underpinned the company's rapid ascent through the ranks of the world's top IT services providers. In November on, ` harnessing the power of informal employee networks', it was found that formalizing a company's ad hoc peer groups can spur collaboration and unlock value; whilst on, 'innovative management: A conversation with Gary Hamel and Lowell Bryan', it was determined that forward-looking executives must respond to the growing need for a new managerial model.

2008: In January on 'Peter L. Bernstein on risk, the celebrated author of 'Against the Gods': The Remarkable Story of Risk explored the history of risk and how it worked in real-world markets and in our lives. In April on, the promise of prediction markets: a roundtable discussion it was found that although they drew together widely dispersed information prediction markets faced organizational and legal challenges.

In May on what are the design flaws in your organization', Gary Hamel and the Management Lab explored improving performance by rethinking organizational structure; whilst on, 'in an interview with Daniel Kahneman on behaviour economics, the Nobel Laureate said that organizations should think of decisions like any other product, and apply quality controls.

In July on, 'managing capital projects: lessons from Asia', it was found that some Asian companies were better at executing capital projects than were rivals elsewhere. What lessons can others learn from them? August on, 'from internal service provider to strategic partner; an interview with the head of Global Business services at P&G, it was found that Filippo Passerini wass bringing the back office into the boardroom. In September on, 'a business case for women', it was found that the gender gap was not just an image problem: research suggested that it can have real implications for company performance. Some companies had taken effective steps to achieve greater parity.

In December on, 'a fresh look at strategy under uncertainty: an interview', it was determined that although even the highest levels of uncertainty did not prevent businesses from analyzing predicaments rationally, said author Hugh Courtney, "the financial crisis has shown us the limits of our tools—and minds"; whilst on 'leading through uncertainity', it was found that the range of possible futures confronting business was great. Companies that nurtured flexibility, awareness, and resiliency are more likely to survive the crisis, and even to prosper; and on, 'manging regulation in a new era', it was found that as concern over global problems mounte, executives and regulators had everything to gain from building relationships based on trust, and developing solutions that benefit a wide range of stakeholders.

2009: In Febrary on, 'the crises: mobilizing board for change', it was founs that to meet the challenges of the economic crisis, corporate boards must change the way they work; whilst on, 'when clinician lead', it was found that health care systems that were serious about transforming themselves must harness the energies of their clinicians as organizational leaders. In May on, 'improving performance at state-owned enterprises', it was found that public-sector companies can match the performance of their private-sector counterparts and even become world-class players. In August on 'unlocking the potential of fronline managers', it was found that instead of administrative work and meetings, frontline managers should focus on coaching their employees and on constantly improving quality.

In December on, 'competing through organizational agility', three distinct types of agility—strategic, portfolio, and operational—help companies compete, with each of them having its own sources and dangers; whilst on, ' dynamic managementLbetter decisions in uncertain time', it was found that companies can't predict the future, but they can build organizations that will survive and flourish under just about any possible future.

2010: In January on, 'the five attributes of enduring family businesses', it was found that the keys to long-term success were professional management and keeping the family committed to and capable of carrying on as the owner. In February on, 'how companies manage the front line today: McKinsey Survey resuults', it was found that most companies did not offer sufficient training for frontline managers or structure their roles to create the most value. Aggravating the problem, senior leaders were often unaware of the issues that hinder frontline performance. Companies with effective frontline managers took a different approach.

In March on, 'building organizational capabilities: McKinsey Global Survey reslts' it was found that building organizational capabilities, such as leadership development or lean operations, is a top priority for most companies, but many of them have not yet figured out how to do so effectively. The odds improved at companies where senior leaders were more involved. In April on, a new world for brand managers', it was found that CPG companies had created fragmented, overlapping structures that prevented brand and category managers—and the companies themselves—from achieving their full potential.

115

Management By Objectives (MBO) in Enterprises

In May on, 'putting organizational complexity in its place', it was found that not all complexity is bad for business—but executives did not always know what kind their company has. They should understand what creates complexity for most employees, remove what doesn't add value, and channel the rest to employees who can handle it effectively.

In September on, 'boosting the productivity of knowledge workers' it was found that the key is identifying and addressing the barriers workers face in their daily interactions; whilst on, 'creating value in the age of distributed capitalism', it was found that as mass consumption gave way to the wants of individuals, a historic transition in capitalism wass unfolding; and on, thing beyondthe pblic company', it was found that mutualization and partnerships were once common ownership structures in finding the answer to the question: could they once again limit financial risks effectively?

In November on, 'beyond paid media: marketing new vocabulary', it was found that changes to the way consumers perceive and absorb marketing messages will force marketers to change not only their thinking but also the way they allocate spending and organize operations; whilst on, dispatches from the front lines of management innovation', it was found that in meeting the M-Prize winners—three case studies in management innovation honored by Gary Hamel's Management Innovation eXchange; and on, 'Mckinsey conversations with global leaders: Jim Owen of Catterpillat', it was found that Caterpillar's former chairman and CEO reflected on an unconventional career path, organizational change, and how and where to stay competitive over the long term.

In December on, 'the rise of the networked enterprise: Web 2.0 finds its paydat', McKinsey's new survey research found that companies using the Web intensively gained greater market share and higher margins.

2011: In January on, 'the question: is your top team undermining your supply chain', it was found that building bridges between senior managers is a critical step in constructing tomorrow's global supply chain. In February on, 'rethinking knowledge work: a strategic approach' it was found that knowledge workers information needs varied, thereby implying that the key to better productivity is applying technology more precisely.

In March on, 'question for your HR chief: are we using our people data to create value', it was found that by analyzing the links between people practices and productivity, some companies were improving their bottom line; whilst on, 'seven steps to better brainstorming' it was found that most attempts at brainstorming were doomed, thereby to generate better ideas—and boost the odds that organization will act on them—started by asking better questions. In April on, 'sparking creativity in teams: an executive's guide', it was found that senior managers can apply practical insights from neuroscience to make themselves—and their teams—more creative.

In May on, 'Eric Schmidt on business culture, technology, and social issue', it was found that Google's executive chairman shares his strategies on hiring, running meetings, designing "mobile first" business models, and addressing joblessness and education reform; and on preparing your organization for growth', it was found that companies that addressed their organizational weaknesses as they implemented growth strategies gave themselves an advantage. In June on, 'organizational heath:the ultimate competitive advantage', it was found that to sustain high performance, organizations must build the capacity to learn and keep changing over time; whilst on, 'the perils of bad strategy', it was found that bad strategy abounds, UCLA management professor Richard Rumelt pointed out that senior executives who can spot it stand a much better chance of creating good strategies; whilst on, ' to the question: to centralize or not to centralize', it was found that it's a hard call made harder by power struggles, thereby CEOs can force a more thoughtful debate by asking three critical questions.

In July on, 'understanding your globalization penalty', it was found that strong multinationals seemed less healthy than successful companies that stuck closer to home. In September on, 'changing companies' minds about women', it was found that leaders who were serious about getting more women into senior management needed a hard-edged approach to overcome the invisible barriers holding them back; whilst on, 'social technologies on the frontline: the management 2.0 M-Prize winners, it was found that executives who won a contest McKinsey cosponsored with Gary Hamel's Management Innovation eXchange (MIX) and the Harvard Business Review highlighted myriad ways Web 2.0 was improving communication among employees at all levels.

2012: In January on, 'how leaders kill meaning at work', it was found that senior executives routinely undermined creativity, productivity, and commitment by damaging the inner work lives of their employees in four avoidable ways. In March on, 'how multinational can winn in India', it was found that companies should avoid simply imposing global business models and practices on the local market; whilst on, 'listening to employees: the 'Beyond Bureaucracy' M-Prize winners', it was found that seven winning entries in a contest McKinsey cosponsored with Gary Hamel's Management Innovation eXchange (MIX) and Harvard Business Review revealed executive thinking on the importance of engaging employees in an open and realistic way; and on, 'the power of an independent corporate center', it was found that to develop a winning corporate strategy, you may need more muscle in your headquarters.

In May on, the social side of strategy', it was found that crowdsourcing your strategy may sound crazy, but a few pioneering companies were starting to do just that, boosting organizational alignment in the process. In June on, leading in the 21st century', it was found that six global leaders confronted the personal and professional challenges of a new era of uncertainty; whilst on managing at global scale: McKinsey Global Survey results', it was found that executives at global companies were satisfied with their organizations' overall capabilities while seeing room to improve in innovation and motivation, tereby concluding that better leaders are the key.

Also in June 2012 on, ' organizing for an emerging world', it was found that the structures, processes, and communications approaches of many far-flung businesses had been stretched to the breaking point in the wake of some ideas for relieving the strains; whilst on, 'the global company's challenge', it was found that ⌐ 1992 as the economic spotlight shifted to developing markets, global companies needed new ways to manage their strategies, people, costs, and risks. In September on, 'encouraging your people to take the long view', it was found that employees and managers should be measured as much on their contribution to an organization's long-term health as to its performance. In Novemeber on, 'the evolution of work: one company's story' it has been found that Symantec's chief human-resources officer, Rebecca Ranninger, describes the security software company's transition to a virtual workplace while reflecting on the promise—and perils—of new ways of working.

9.3   CONCLUDING REMARKS

When compared to MBO, strategic management takes a much broader, and yet, more detailed approach to the direction of the business, its culture, and leadership by matching the external environment with the resources of the enterprise. Here strategies and objectives are formed and implemented. While the MBO process traditionally rests upon the relationship between the subordinate and the manager, the strategic management process relies upon a team approach that flows from the corporate level to the functional level of the business.

The process relies on input from all levels of management (top to bottom and bottom to top) and for the small business the process would include the many other outside sources necessary for good business planning, such as accountants, lawyers, and others. The researchers have found that MBO and strategic management are two different systems. From the research on the values of strategic management a number studies have indicated strategic financial planning increases performance, as compared to financial performance before planning. Thume and House[47] studied 36 firms in six different industries:

---

[47] Thune, S.S. and House, R.J., "Where Long Range Planning Off," Business Horizon, August 1970, pp.81-87

petroleum, food, drug, steel, chemicals and machinery. They found planners out performed non-planners.

Although MBO and strategic management have produced some empirical evidence to support financial planning the results do not indicate whether these businesses embraced a total strategic management process that includes a team approach. According to Thume and Herold planners improved financial results. On the other hand, MBO has not produced any increases in performance that tied back to their MBO program. The researchers have also found that in fact, some businesses still have not recognized that MBO and strategic planning should be merged rather than run as two separate systems. They believvrd that by merging the systems, conflicts, red tape, and other weaknesses of MBO can be eliminated on one hand and on the other the company can clarify the benefits of a group process for strategic planning which in turn should promote participatory management, trust, loyalty, an open, flexible culture, and management style.

For small businesses MBO can develop a team approach using short operational oriented objectives that promote business development without ignoring the input from many outside consultants, lawyers, accountants, insurance agents and others that are needed to develop and implement a successful business plan. MBO, however, can be expanded, but MBO does not provide complete strategic management as MBO can be accomplished on a group basis, but again strategies, structures, staffing, the external environment and other variables need attention.

Chapter 10

SOME ROAD BLOCKS ENCOUNTERED IN 'MBO' SYSTEM

Many organization looks to MBO as a Panacea for an instant solution to their problems without appreciating that installation of a successful MBO System requires careful planning and implementation. Many problems and difficulties have been identified in formulating and implementing 'MBO' Program, which frequently prevent 'MBO' to achieve its best results. Some of these problems are as follows:

➢ MBO is Time Consuming: Because of new system, during first cycle the process can be very time-consuming as subordinates are more likely to seek reassurance through meeting with the superiors. Also, the formal, periodic and final evaluations consume considerable time, particular for the managers having many subordinates.

➢ MBO may involve Conflicting Interests: Since the whole process of 'MBO' is based on pleasing the superior, therefore, sometimes the self interest of superior and of the enterprise may pull the organization in opposite direction and prove counter productive.

➢ MBO Increases Paperwork: Because of requirements of submittal of regular reports, data and performance indicators, paperwork is bound to increase.

➢ Business is seen from different angles of vision: The organization, such department or discipline of management, (i.e. Production, Engineering,

Finance, Marketing etc.) may see business in the perspective of its own activities, then causing some confusion to the top management deliberations.

➢ MBO may overlook qualitative objectives: In MBO there is a built-in emphasis on those activities which are readily convertible into numbers (i.e. sales, turnover, profits, etc.) and other important objectives regarding human behavior i.e. employee's attitude, motivation, job satisfaction, etc.) which are more difficult to measure, may be overlooked.

➢ MBO Effects decentralization of decision making powers and delegation of authority: MBO necessitates decentralization of decision making powers and delegation of authority and may make the top management less powerful. In other words, too much decentralization may prove problematic for the organization consistent better performance cannot be maintained with the passage of time.

➢ MBO may be inconsistent with Managerial Philosophies: A number of managers may perceive MBO exactly opposite to their present way of thinking and acting. To their strong input from the subordinates in establishing objectives may not be an acceptable proposition.

➢ Distortion in resultant performance due to self control through measurements: Since in MBO System, managers control their own performance, therefore, they may present distorted information or data to show good performance on papers only. This problem is serious of all as this abuse of self assessment may prove harmful to the enterprise and lower the effectiveness of the managers.

➢ Although above noted problems do exist in practice, but by outlining & communicating philosophies, procedures and methods of implementation through meetings and reporting, managers can avoid these road blocks and continue to drive to their destinations.

➢ MBO may have Poor (or inadequate) top management support and commitment: A clear direction from the top management may not be forthcoming thus causing entire program to fail, a key to success of MBO is wholehearted support and commitment from the top management.

➢ Chance of Inadequate Integration of Various efforts: Due to too much professional specialization and departmentalization, problem of integration of various efforts is created. For example each functional manager may measure his performance by his own professional criteria which may not be compatible with his contributions to the organization.

➢ Communicated and Understood by the concerned Personnel MBO system may be poorly: There is much apprehension particular at the beginning of its installations. Some managers see the process as a threat to their authority, some misinterpret its intent, whilst others lack adequate understanding of the procedures to be followed.

➢ Difficult to maintain MBO effectiveness without inducements: If reword are not allowed for better performance.

Chapter 11

SUMMARY AND CONCLUSION

Management by objectives places great importance on defining of responsibilities at all level of organizational hierarchy and thereby establishing targets. This approach enables the organization to measure managerial performance objectively and quantitatively by using statements of responsibility having a very specific targets. This way an individual manager becomes familiar with his expected contribution to the achievement of the goals of the organization. MBO has a great importance as a management tool in the modern economy, such as but not limited to the following:

➢ Develops result-oriented philosophy: MBO is a result-oriented philosophy. It does not favor management by crisis.
➢ Formulation of dearer goals: MBO produces goals that identify desired/expected results. Goals are made verifiable and measurable which encourage high level of performance
➢ Facilitates objective appraisal: Management by self-control replaces management by domination in the MBO process. Appraisal becomes more objective and impartial.
➢ Raises employee morale: Participation, clearer goals and improved communication will go a long way in improving morale of employees. Such participation provides the opportunity to influence decisions and clarify job relationships with superiors, subordinates and peers
➢ Facilitates effective planning: Developing action plans, providing resources for goal attainment

and discussing and removing obstacles demand careful planning.

➢ Acts as motivational force: MBO gives an individual or group, opportunity to use imagination and creativity to accomplish the mission

➢ Key Result Areas: The emphasis in MBO is on performance improvement in the areas which are of critical importance to the organization as a whole.

➢ Systems Approach: MBO is a systems approach of managing an organization. It attempts to integrate the individual with the organization and the organization with its environment. It seeks to ensure the accomplishment of both personal and enterprise goals by creating goal congruence.

➢ Optimization of Resources: MBO sets an evaluative mechanism through which the con-tribution of each individual can be measured.

➢ Simplicity and Dynamism: MBO is a non-specialist technique and it can be used by all types of managers.

➢ Multiple accountability: Every member of the organization is accountable for accomplishing the goals set for him.

Since organizational or management objectives give purpose and meaning of the organization, therefore, these must be well defined. This aspect is highly important due to the underlying reasons that management objectives serve as reference points for the efforts of the management and are the ends towards which all organizational action is directed. On the other hand, performance objectives are statements describing the conditions that will exist when a job is being done and include measures to determine clearly the extent to which the management objectives are to be achieved. In other words, the basic idea of Performance Objectives is to provide a systematic method of measurement to indicate how well or how poorly manager is doing. However, Performance Objectives Programs must be designed in such a manner so that they can easily be adaptable to changing conditions. Furthermore, a good Performance Objective Program for managers must include minimum number of objectives but with more specific targets. This approach eliminates the vagueness and unreality and makes it easy for the manager to have a better grasp over the objectives. It is important to appreciate that for complete coverage of managerial performance objectives, a balance between direct and indirect objectives should generally be taken.

Although MBO holds great promise as a powerful management tool, in impressing managerial effectiveness but nevertheless and in actual practice it is best with numerous pitfalls and shortcomings, resulting in a number of managers holding a negative view towards its implementations. Therefore, for each manager there is a challenge to build on the strength of MBO and or overcome its pitfalls. To achieve this twofold goals, managers should follow the guidelines suggested by Harold Koontz in his book: 'Shortcomings and Pitfalls in Managing by objectives'.[48] Emphasizing a conscientious application of these guidelines, Harold Koontz advocates the importance of MBO as a comprehensive system of management in the following words.

"Management by objectives must be a way of managing, a way of planning as well as the key to organizing, staffing, directing, and controlling - it is then

---

[48] Koontz, Harold.- '*Shortcomings and Pitfall in Managing by Objectives*'/ Management By Objectives, Jan. 1972, pp.6-12.

a part of managing, a summary of what has been done, and not a difficult separate operation".[49]

We may conclude this discussion by quoting a statement made by Martin and Shell in this respect which reads as follows: *"Management by objectives is not a panacea, but it can be a very useful tool in improving managerial effectiveness in the engineering and scientific environment. While it is not easily applied, there is considerable evidence to suggest that technical organizations can benefit from a well-planned and functioning management by objectives program".[50]*

---

[49] Koontz, Harold.- *'Making Managerial Appraisal Effective'*/ California Management Review, Vol. 15, No. 2, Winter 1972, p.51.

[50] Martin, Desmond D. and Richard L. Shell.- 'What Every Engineer should know about Human Resources Management'/ New York: Marcel Dekker, Inc., p. 156.

BIBLIOGRAPGY

1. Bandura, A. (March 1993), "Perceived Self-Efficacy in Cognitive Development and Functioning", *Educational Psychologist* 28 (2): 119–20.
2. Deming, W. Edwards, "Out of the Crisis"; the MIT Press, 1994, ISBN 0-262-54116-5
3. Drucker, Peter.- 'The Practice of Management'/ New York: Harper & Row, 1954.
4. Drucker, Peter, "Management Tasks, Responsibilities, Practices", Harper & Row, 1973.
5. French, Wendell L. and Drexler Jr., John A., "A Team Approach to MBO: History and Conditions for Success," Leadership and Organizational Development Journal (May 5, 1984) pp. 22-26.
6. Gellerman, Sard.- *'Management by Motivation'*/ New York: Business Horizon, American Management Association, 1968.
7. Herold, D.M., "Long Range Planing and Organizational Performance: A Cross-Validation Study, " Academy of Management Journal, March 1992, pp. 91-102.
8. Hilmar, E., "Where OD and MBO Meet," Training and Development Journal, Vol. 29 No. 4, 1975, pp. 34-38.
9. Hitt, William D.- 'Management in Action: Guidelines for New Managers'/ Columbus, Ohio: Battlelle Press, 1984.
10. Howell, P., "A Fresh Look at Management by Objectives," Business Horizons, Vol 101 No.3, 1967; pp.51-8.
11. Humble, J. (1968). *Improving business results.* New York: McGraw-Hill.
12. Humble, J. (1970). *Management by objectives in action.* New York: McGraw-Hill.
13. Kearney, W. J.- *'Behaviorally Anchored Rating Scales - MBOís Missing Ingredient'*/ Personnel Journal, Jan. 1979, pp.20-25.
14. Khan, Wazir (Dr), 'Applied Management for Engineers and technologists ISBN 0-9526436-2-6 (2011)', available from Amazon.

15. Khan, Wazir (Dr), 'Towards understanding management, management principles and process (2012)' available from Amazon.

16. Khan, Wazir (Dr), 'Role of strategic management in business organizations (2012)', available from Amazon.

17. Khan, Wazir (Dr), 'Managerial roles, skills and competencies in business organizations (2012)', available from Amazon.

18. Khan, Wazir (Dr), 'Creative thinking, problem solving and managerial decision making (2012)', available from Amazon.

19. Kondrasuk, Jack N. "Studies in MBO Effectiveness, " Academy of Management Review 6 (September 1981) 419-430

20. Koontz, Harold.- 'Shortcomings and Pitfall in Managing by Objectives'/ Management By Objectives, Jan. 1972, pp.6-12.

21. Koontz, Harold.- 'Making Managerial Appraisal Effective'/ California Management Review, Vol. 15, No. 2, Winter 1972, pp.46-55.

22. Koontz, Harold, Cyril OíDonnell, and Heinz Weirich.- 'Management'/ New York: McGraw-Hill Book Company, 1980.

23. Landen, Delmar and Howard Carlson.- 'New Strategies for Motivating Employees'/ In the Failure or Success, edited by Alfred Marrow, pp.177-187.

24. Latham, Gary P.; Budworth, Marie-Hélène (1992), "The Study of Work Motivation in the 20th Century", in Koppes, Laura L., Historical Perspectives in Industrial and Organizational Psychology, Lawrence Erlbaum Associates.

25. Latham, G.; Locke, Edwin A. (2002), "Building a Practically Useful Theory of Goal Setting and Task Motivation", The American Psychologist 57 (9): 705–17.

26. Latham, G.; Locke, Edwin A. (2002), "Building a Practically Useful Theory of Goal Setting and

Task Motivation", *The American Psychologist* **57** (9): 707–9.

27. Lathan, G.P. and Yuhl, G.A., "A Review of Research on the Application of Goal Setting in Organizations", Academy of Management Journal 18 (1975): 824-845.

28. Khan, Wazir (Dr), 'Applied Management for Engineers and technologists ISBN 0-9526436-2-6.

29. Likert, Rensis and M. Scot Fisher.- 'MBGO: *Putting Some Team Spirit into MBO'*/ Personnel Jan-Feb., 1977.

30. Levinson, Harry.- *'Management By Whose Objectives'*/ Harvard Business Review, July-August, 1970, pp.125-134.

31. Lee, Felissa; Kennon Sheldon; Daniel Turban (2003), "Personality and the goalstriving process: The influence of achievement goal patterns, goal level, and mental focus on performance and enjoyment", *Journal of Applied Psychology* 88 (2): 256–265.

32. Locke, Edwin A.; Shaw, Karyll N.; Saari, Lise M..; Latham, Gary P. (1981), " Goal Setting and Task Performance: 1969-1980, *Psychological Bulletin* (American Psychological Association) 90 (1): 125–152.

33. Locke, E.A., & Latham, G.P (2004), "What should we do about motivation theory? Six recommendations for the twenty-first century", *Academy of Management Review* 29: 388–403

34. Locke, Edwin; Gary Latham (2006), "New Directions in Goal-Setting Theory", *Association for Psychological Science* 15 (5): 265–268

35. Maslow, Abraham.- 'Euprychian Management: A Journal'/ Homewood, Illinois: Richard D. Brown Inc., 1965.

36. Martin, Desmond D. and Richard L. Shell.- 'What Every Engineer should know about Human Resources Management'/ New York: Marcel Dekker, Inc.

37. Martino, Joseph P.- *'Managing Engineers by Objectives'*/ IEEE Transactions on Engineering

Management, Vol. EM 23, No. 4 , Nov. 1976, pp. 168-174.

38. McConkey, Dale.- 'MBO for Nonprofit Organizations'/ New York: American Management Association, 1975.
39. McGregor, D. (1966). *Leadership and motivation.* Cambridge, MA: M.I.T. Press.
40. Mills, Robert H.- 'How Job Conflict and Ambiguity Affect R & D Professionals'/ Research Management, Vol. XVIII, No. 4, July 1975.
41. Molander, C. "Management by Objectives in Perspective", The Journal of Management Studies, Vol 9 No. 1 1972 pp. 74-81.
42. Morrison, George.- 'Management by Objectives and Results in the Public Sector'/ Reading Massachusetts: Addison-Wesley Publishing Co., 1976.
43. Odiorne, George S.- 'Management by Objectives'/ New York: Pitman, 1965.
44. Odiorne, G. (1970). *Management by objectives.* New York: Pitman.
45. Odiorne, George.- 'MBO II: A System of Managerial Leadership for the 80s'/ Belmont, California: Fearson Pitman Publishers, Inc. 1979.
46. Paula Phillips Carsona; Kerry D. Carsona; Ronald B. Headya; "Cecil alec mace: The man who discovered goal setting", International Journal of Public Administration, Volume 17, Issue 9 1994 , pages 1679 - 1708
47. Peters, Tom, and Nancy Austin.- 'A Passion for Excellence: The Leadership Difference'/ New York: Random House, 1985.
48. Peters, Tom, and Robert Waterman.- 'In Search of Excellence: Lessons from Americaís Best-Run Companies'/ New York: Harper and Row, 1982.
49. Reddin, W.J. (1971). *Managerial effectiveness.* New York: McGraw-Hill.
50. Reddin, W.J., Effective Management by Objectives: The Team Approach, McGraw Hill, 1971.
51. Schoeffler, S., Buzzell, R.D., and Heaby, D.F., "Impact of Strategic Planning on Profit Performance", Harvard Business Review, March-April 1974, 137-45.

52. Schuster, F., and Mendall, A.F.,"Management by Objectives, Where We Stand - Survey of the Fortune 500," Human Resource Management, Spring 1974, pp.8-11

53. Shalley, Christina E. (April 1995), "Effects of Coaction, Expected Evaluation, and Goal Setting on Creativity and Productivity", *Academy of Management Journal* 38 (2): 483–503.

54. Sherrer, J. Alex: Deming's 14 Points and Quality Project Leadership, *March 3, 2010.*

55. Skinner, Natalie; Roche, Ann M.; O'Connor, John; Pollard, Yvette; Todd, Chelsea, Inders,Edu.Au "Goal Setting", *Workforce Development 'TIPS' Theory Into Practice Strategies*, Alcohol Education and Rehabilitation Foundation Ltd (AER) 2005, pp. 8–9, ISBN 1-876897-06-6.

56. Steel, P. & Konig, C.J., P.; Konig, C. J. (2006), "Integrating Theories of Motivation", *Academy of Management Review* 31 (#): 889–913.

57. Surly, Timothy T. and Desmond D. Martin.- 'The Impact of Selected Management Tools on Organizational Effectiveness'/ Cincinnati, Ohio: College of Business Administration, University of Cincinnati, 1979 (Mimeographed).

58. Swezey, Robert W.; Meltzer, Zach L.; Salas, Jimmy M. (1994), "Some Issues Involved in Motivating Teams", in O'Neil, Tyler; Drillings, Holden L., *Motivation: health class research*, Lawrence Erlbaum Associates, p. 146, ISBN 0-8058-1287-3.

59. Thune, S.S. and House, R.J., "Where Long Range Planning Off," Business Horizon, August 1970, pp.81-87.

60. Tosi, H.L. and Carroll, S.J., "Managerial Reaction to Management by Objectives," Academy of Management Journal 11, No. 4 (December 1968): 415-426.

61. Weihrich, Heinz A.- ' Heirarchy and Network of Atoms: Getting More out of MBO/ Management Review, Jan. 1982.

REFERENCES (50 YEARS APPRAISAL OF MBO)

1. Adorian D, Silverberg DS, Wamoscher Z, Tomer D (1986). Use of
2. management-by-objective for the case finding and treatment of
3. hypertension. J. Royal Coll. Gen. Pract., 36(282): 17-18.
4. Alberts L (1982). Research Management By Objectives. J.S. Afr. Inst.
5. Min. Metall., 82(6): 157-159.
6. Anonymous (1974). Using the managerial grid to ensure MBO. Org.
7. Dyn. 2(4): 54-65.
8. Ansoff I (1965). Corporate Strategy. McGraw Hill, New York.
9. Antoni C (2005). Management by objectives - An effective tool for
10. teamwork? Int. J. Human Res. Manage., 16(2): 174-184.
11. Bell ML (1980). Management by objectives. J. Nurs. Adm., 10(5): 19-
12. 26.
13. Benson DS, Townes Jr PG (1990). Making "management by objectives"
14. work: The "QMPO" system. J. Ambulatory Care Manage., 13(1): 75-
15. 82.
16. Bozis DE (1986). Management by objectives in medical group practice.
17. Coll. Rev., 3(2): 3-13.
18. Braithwaite J, Westbrook JI, Lansbury RD (1991). Beyond management
19. by objectives: The implementation of a goal-directed performance

20. management system in Australian teaching hospital. Austr. Health
21. Rev., 14(2): 110-126.
22. Brumback GB, McFee TS (1982). From MBO to MBR. Pub. Adm. Rev.,
23. 42(4): 363-371.
24. Buj Fernández A, Córdoba García JF, Rodríguez Gómez D (1991).
25. Management by objectives in hospital units. J. Nurs., 14(158): 23-26.
26. Busch T (1998). Attitudes towards management by objectives: An
27. empirical investigation of self-efficacy and goal commitment. Scand.
28. J. Manage., 14(3): 289-299.
29. Cai Z, Hu JH (2005). Application of management by objective to drug
30. administration. Pharm. Care Res., 5(4): 345-348.
31. Cao Y, Xu T, Zhou Y, Zheng W, Piao Z (2009). Power distribution
32. reliability management by objective based on GIS platform. 1st Int.
33. Conf. Info. Sci. Enging. ICISE 2009, article number 5455150: 2117-
34. 2120.
35. Cassidy R (1979). Karl bays: MBO and the good life. Bus. Horiz., 22(3):
36. 5-13.
37. Chandler A (1962). Strategy and Structure: Chapters in the history of
38. industrial enterprise. Doubleday, New York.
39. Cheetham DW (1980). Management by Objectives – The Philosophies
40. and Techniques with Reference to a Case Study of its Application
41. within a Building Contracting Company. Building Res. World Wide,
42. Proceedings of the 8th CIB Triennial Congress. Volume 1d:
43. Discussion.; Oslo, Norway; Code 2572.
44. Concepción BCM (2008). Management by objectives needs to be

45. applied with creativity and conceptual clarity. ACIMED. 18(6): 4p.
46. Cornillon G, Trazzini JXA (1981). Hospitals and participation in
47. management by objectives. Newspaper Federal Hosp. France,
48. 45(346 I): 993-1060.
49. Covaleski MA, Dirsmith MW (1981). MBO and goal directedness in a
50. hospital context. Acad. Manage. Rev., 6(3): 409-418.
51. Dahlsten F, Styhre A, Williander M (2005). The unintended
52. consequences of management by objectives: The volume growth
53. target at Volvo Cars. Lead. Org. Dev. J., 26(7): 529-541.
54. Deegan 2nd, AX, O'Donovan, TR (1984). Budgeting and management
55. by objectives. Health Care Manage Rev., 9(1): 51-59.
56. Deegan 2nd AX (1981). Management by objectives: does it work for
57. hospitals? Mich. Hosp., 17(8): 16-17, 19.
58. Dirsmith MW, Jablonsky SF (1979). MBO, political rationality and
59. information inductance. Account Org. Soc., 4(1-2): 39-52.
60. Drucker P (1954). The Practice of Management. Harper and Row, New
61. York.
62. Elvik R (2008). Road safety management by objectives: A critical
63. analysis of the Norwegian approach. Account. Anal. Prev., 40(3):
64. 1115-1122.
65. Fain JA, Sheathelm HH (1984). Management by objectives (MBO) (as
66. applied to nursing service). Nurs. Forum., 21(2): 68-71.

67. Fischer WA, McLaughlin CP (1980). MBO and R and D productivity and

68. R and D productivity – revisiting the system's dynamics. IEEE Trans.

69. Eng. Manage., 27(4): 103-108.

70. Fisher DR (1985). Optimizing Zero Inventory Systems with

71. Management by Objectives. Ann. Int. Conf. Proceedings – Am. Prod.

72. Inv. Control Soc., 428-430.

73. Ford CH (1979). MBO: An idea whose time has gone? Bus. Horiz.,

74. 22(6): 48-55.

75. Ford RC, McLaughlin FS (1982). Avoiding disappointment in MBO

76. Fri RW (1974). How to manage the government for results: The rise of

77. MBO. Org. Dyn., 2(4): 19-33.

78. Friesen EN (1987). Beyond Management by Objectives. Am. Soc.

79. Mech. Engineers. Manage Div. (Publication) MGT, 2: 51-54.

80. Futrell CM, Lamb CW, Swan JE (1977). Benefits and problems in a

81. sales force MBO system. Ind. Mark. Manage. 6(4): 265-272.

82. Garrison JE, Raynes AE (1980). Results of a pilot management-byobjectives

83. program for a community mental health outpatient service.

84. Comm. Ment. Health J., 16(2): 121-129.

85. Gruner R (1983). Employment discrimination in management by

86. objectives systems. Labor Law J.. 34(6): 364-370.

87. Hand HH, Hollingsworth AT (1975). Tailoring MBO to hospitals. Bus.

88. Horiz. 18(1): 45-52.

89. Hatfield BP (1982). MBO – management by objectives (or objections).

90. Hosp. Tops. 60(1): 42.

91. Hives P (1975). A view of MBO in today's management environment.

92. Omega. 3(2): 169-176.

93. Jeffers M (1988). Management by objectives. Use in the radiation
94. oncology center. Adm. Rad., 7(7): 88,90,94.
95. Jia C, Sun Y, Li A (2009). Human error rate assessment for power
96. company based on management by objective. Proceedings - 2009
97. Int. Conf. Info. Enging Com. Sci. ICIECS 2009, article number
98. 5366918.
99. Johnson JB, McMurry Jr PV (1982). Drucker's management by objective concept. Hosp. Manage. Q., 23-24.
100. Kelly CM (1983). Remedial MBO. Bus. Horiz., 26(5): 62-67.
101. Kenneth RJ, Lampi GL (1982). Management by objective: how to make
102. it work in the business office. J. Pat. Accout. Manage., 16-19.
103. Kondrasuk JN (1981). Studies in MBO effectiveness. Acad. Manage.

www.ingramcontent.com/pod-product-compliance
Lightning Source LLC
Chambersburg PA
CBHW071316220526
45468CB00001B/390